I HOPE
I BREAK
EVEN

I COULD
USE THE
MONEY

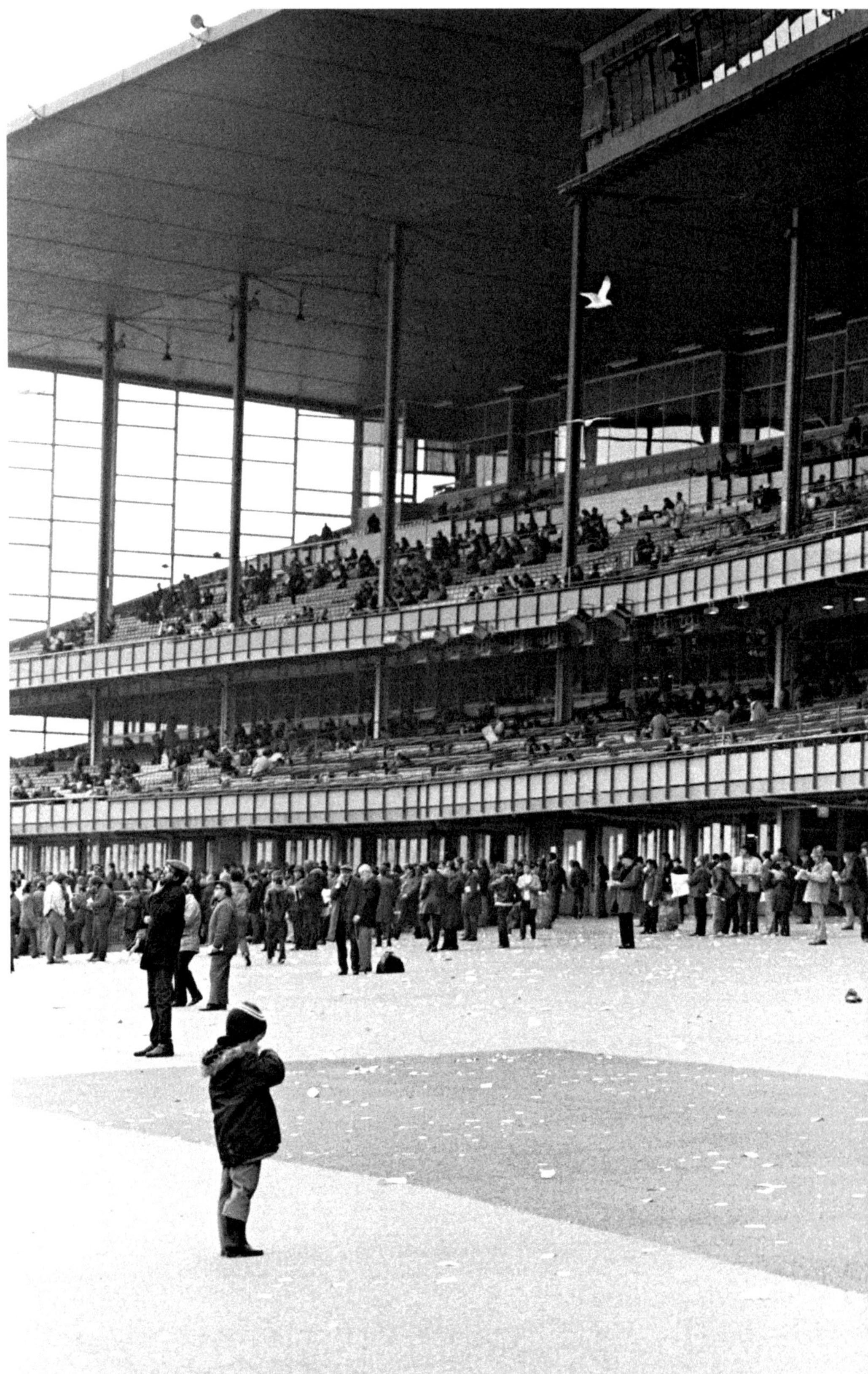

I HOPE I BREAK EVEN

I COULD USE THE MONEY

Photographs from Aqueduct Racetrack, 1972

LARRY RACIOPPO

Essay by JOE BIANCA

Blurring Books

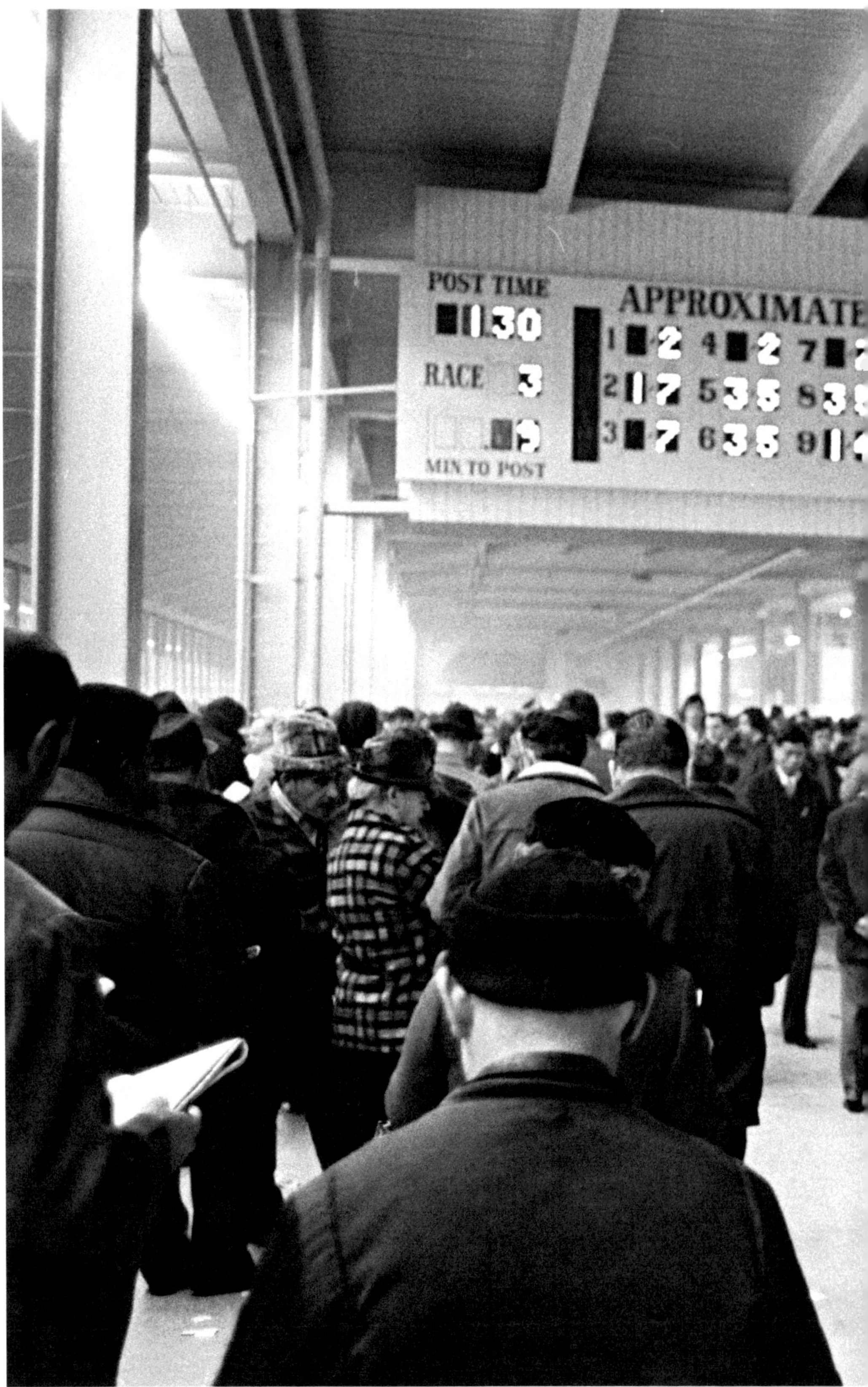

POST TIME
1 30
RACE 3
9
MIN TO POST
APPROXIMATE
1 2 4 2 7
2 7 5 3 5 8 3
3 7 6 3 5 9 2

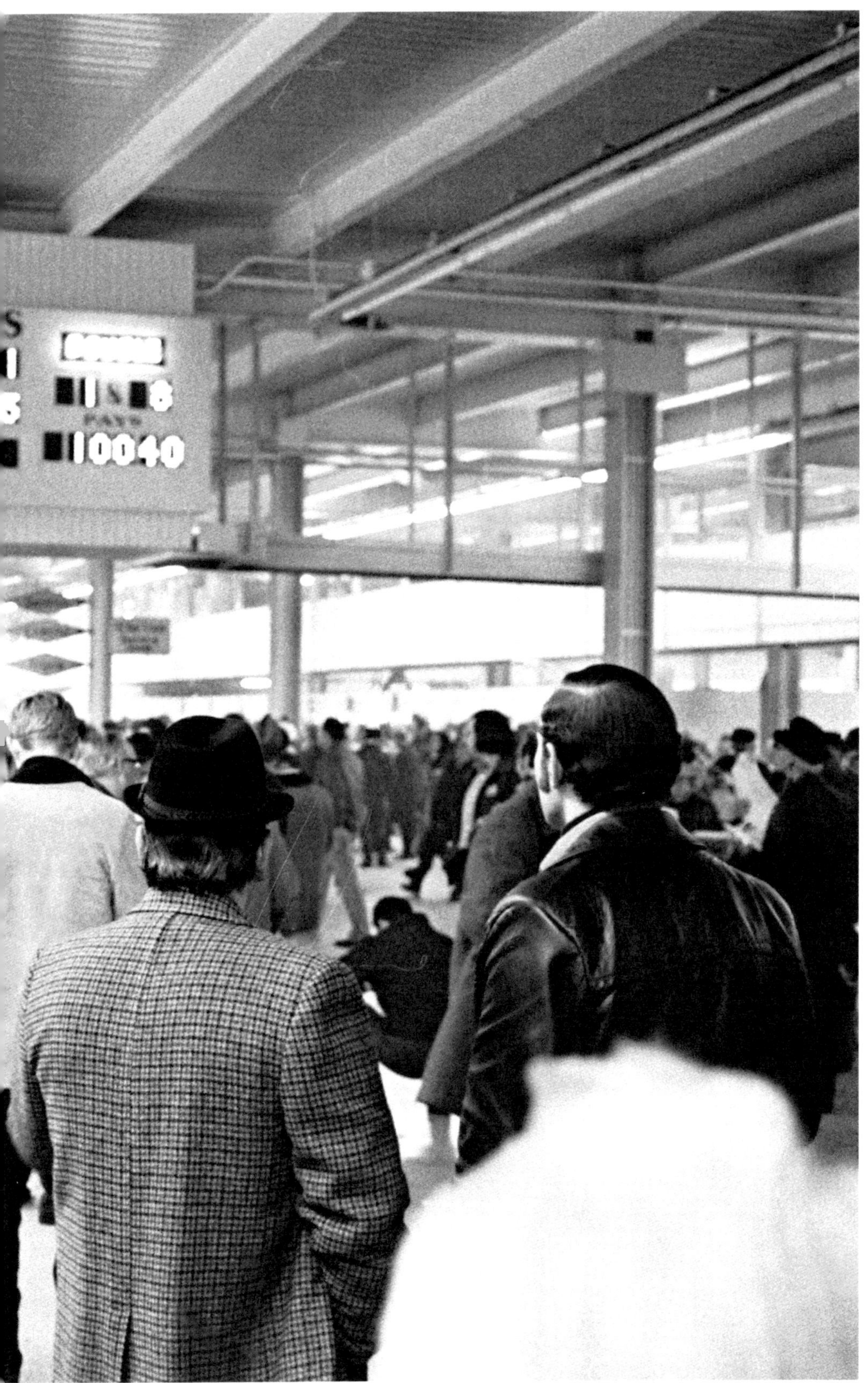
PASS
10040

"I hope I break even, I could use the money."

—Overheard at Aqueduct

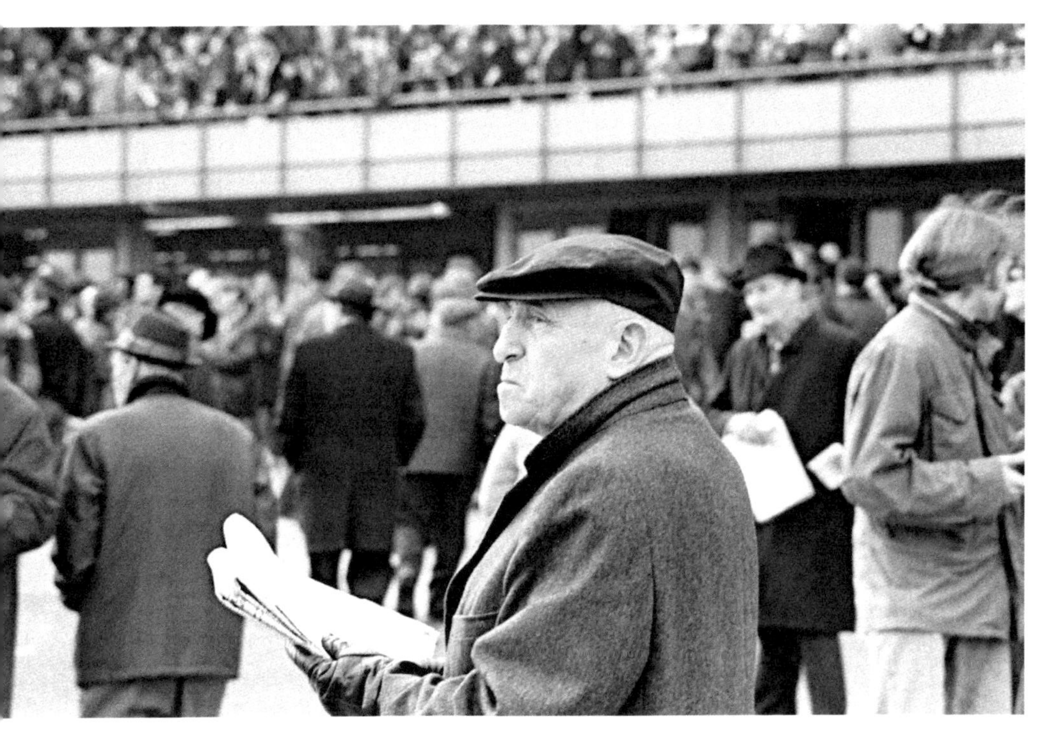

Early in 1972 I went to Aqueduct racetrack with my father and
my Uncle Nick. They had the day off, and I had a new telephoto
lens that I wanted to try out.

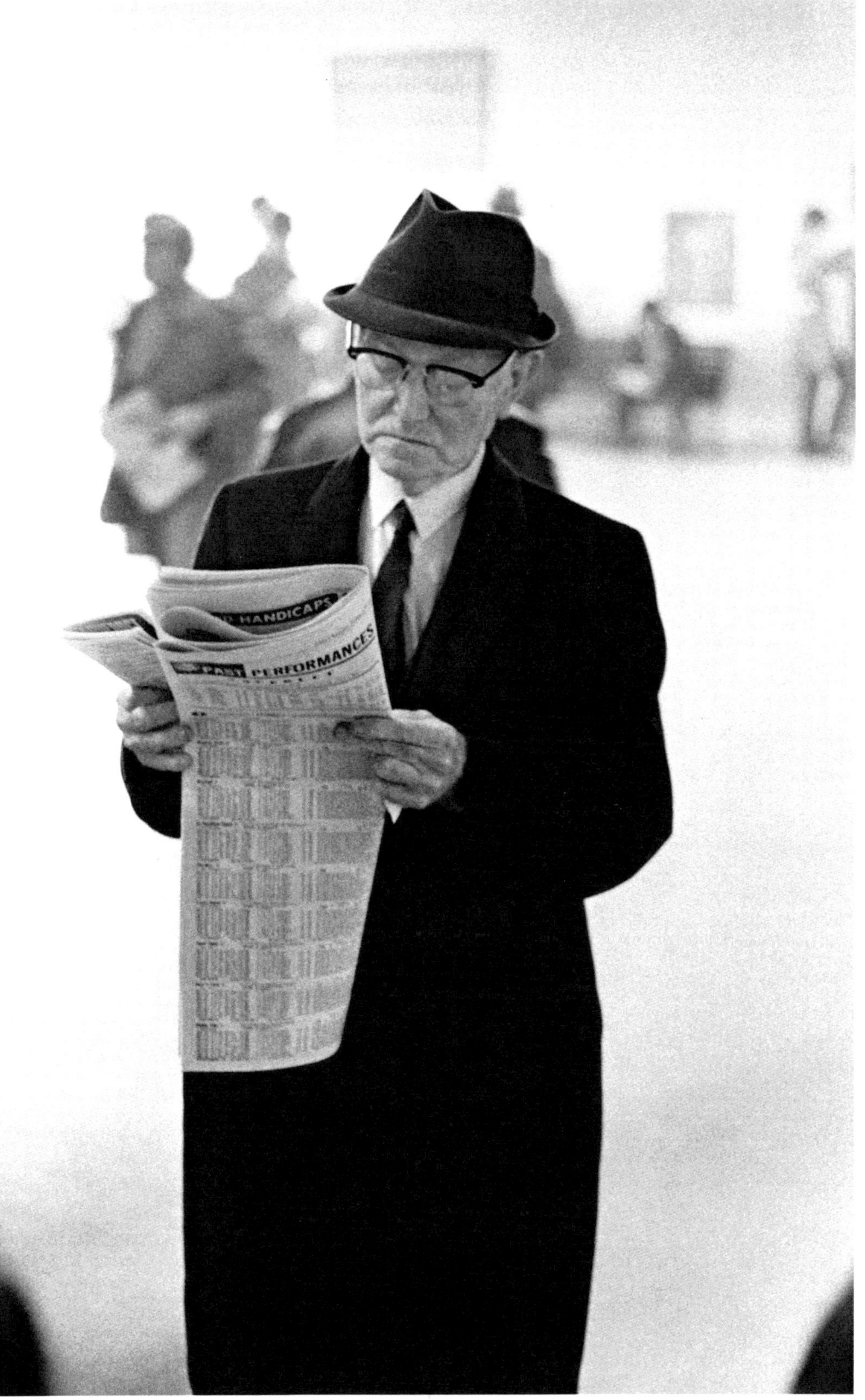
HANDICAPS
PAST PERFORMANCES

I wasn't doing much of anything back then besides occasionally driving a yellow taxi and photographing a bit. I spent the day wandering around the track, taking pictures without asking anyone for permission.

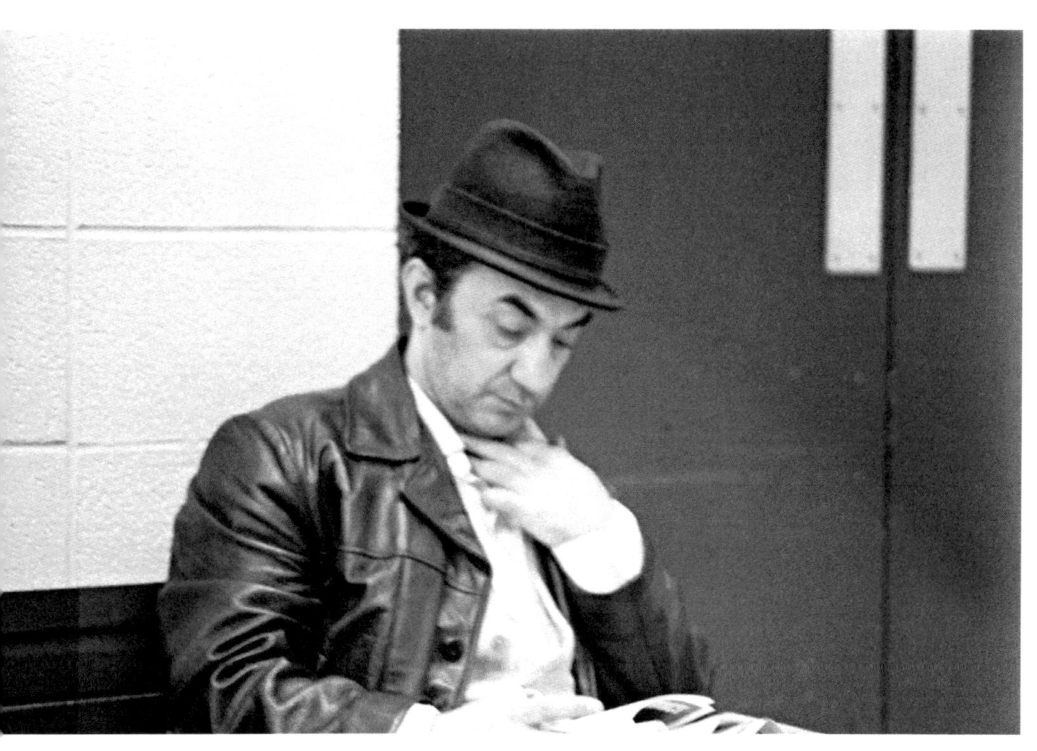

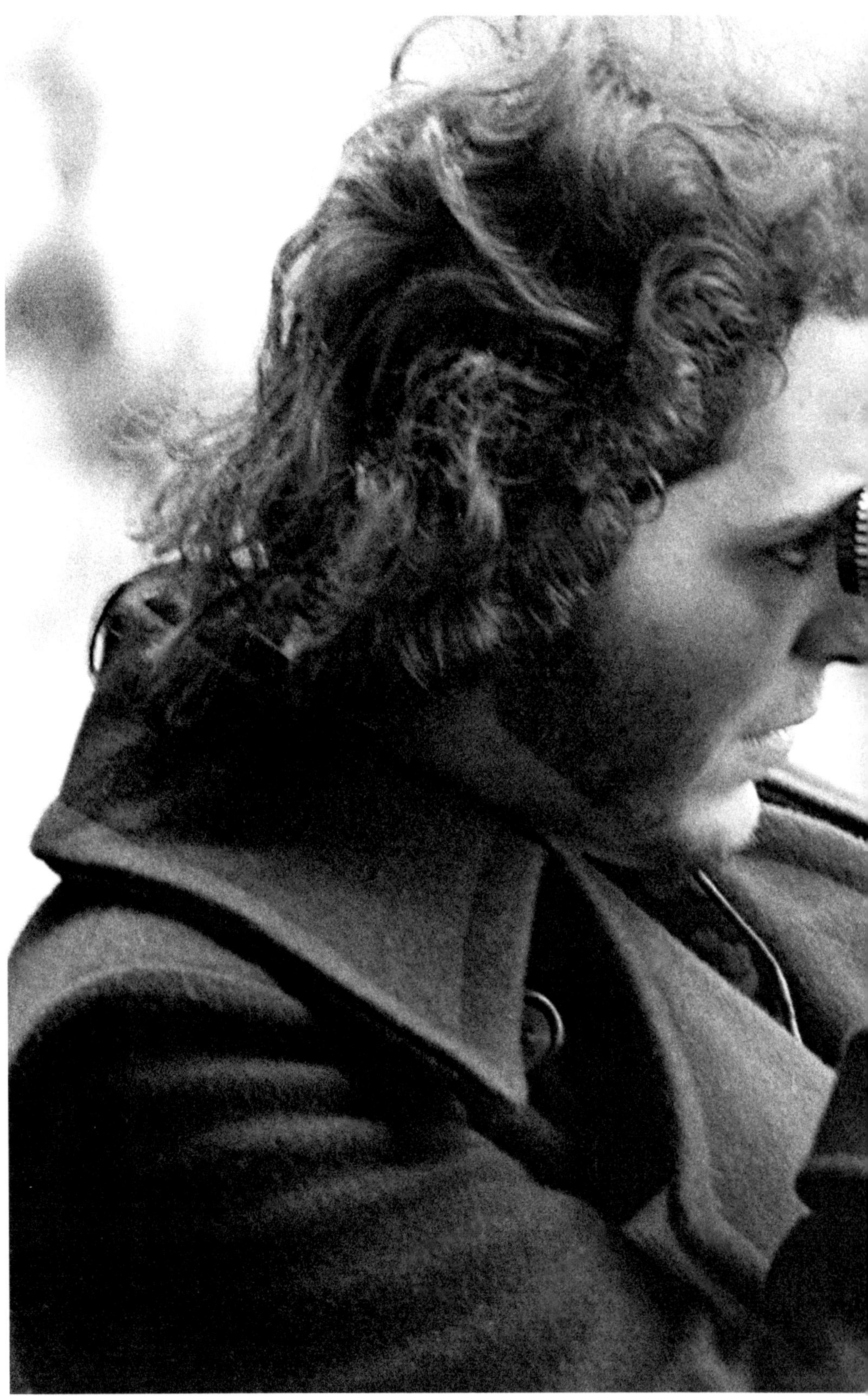

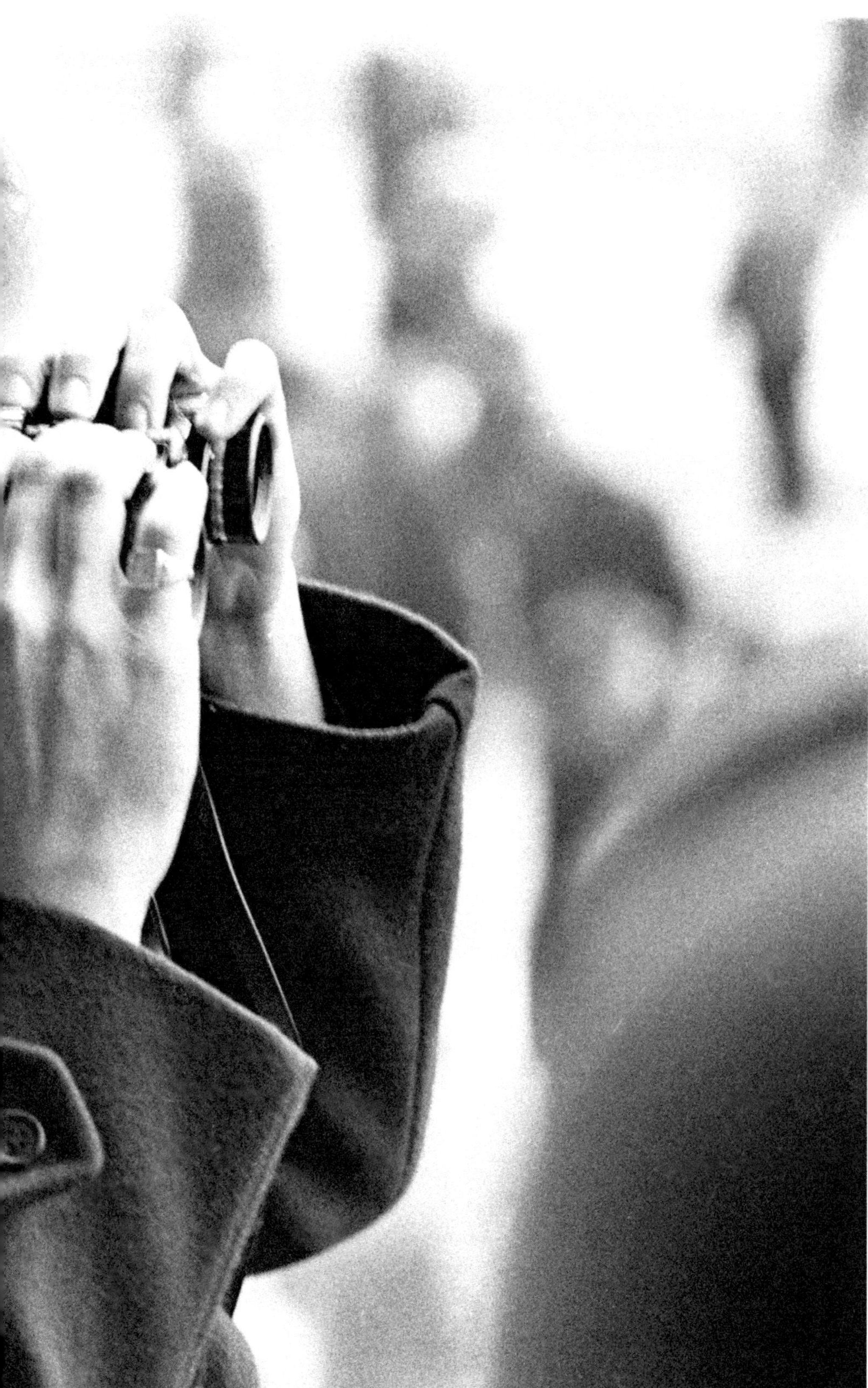

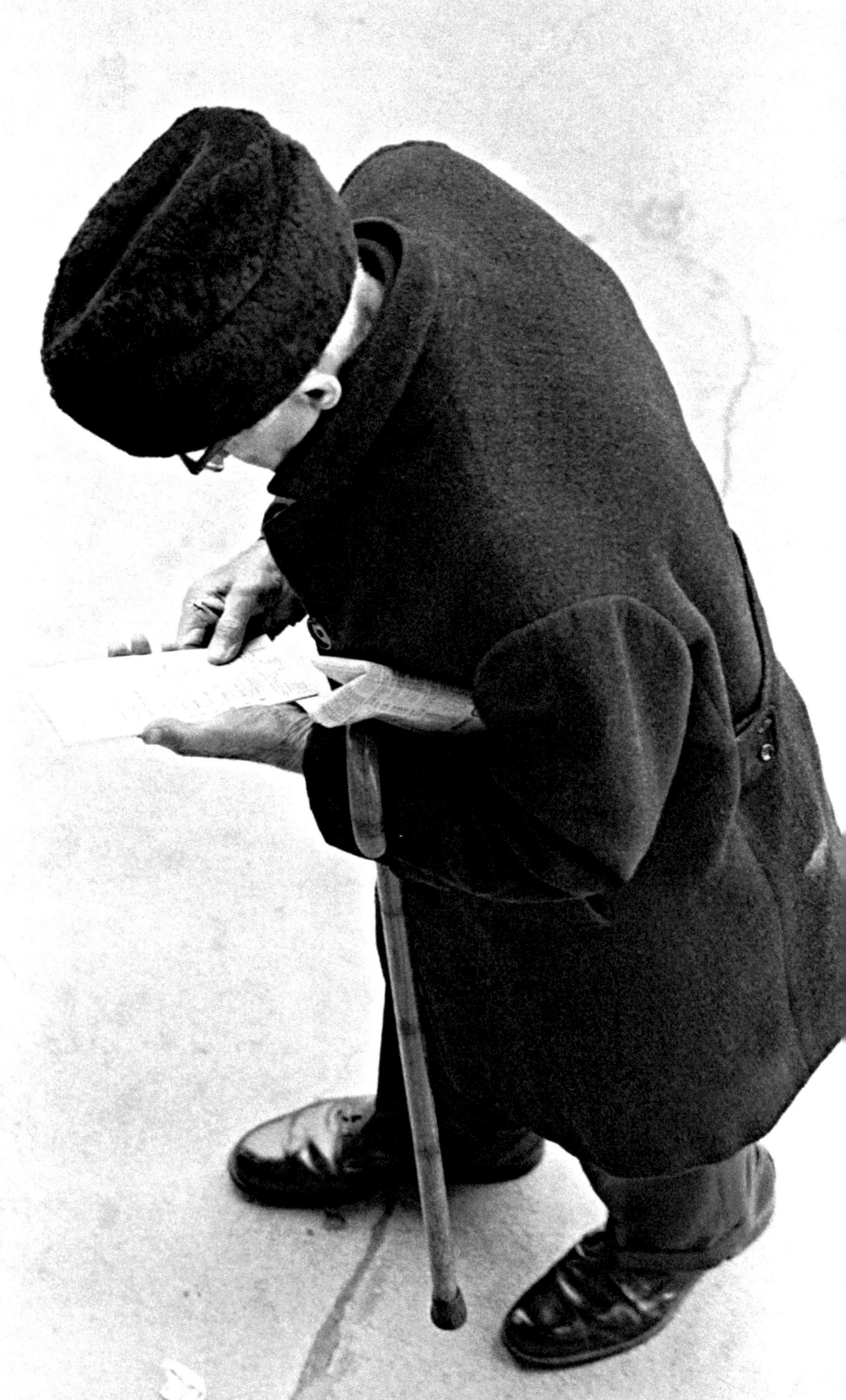

The people at Aqueduct were overwhelmingly white working-class men. A few chatted with people nearby, but most of them stood or squatted alone. They often carried a copy of *The Morning Telegraph* and an Aqueduct program of the day's races.

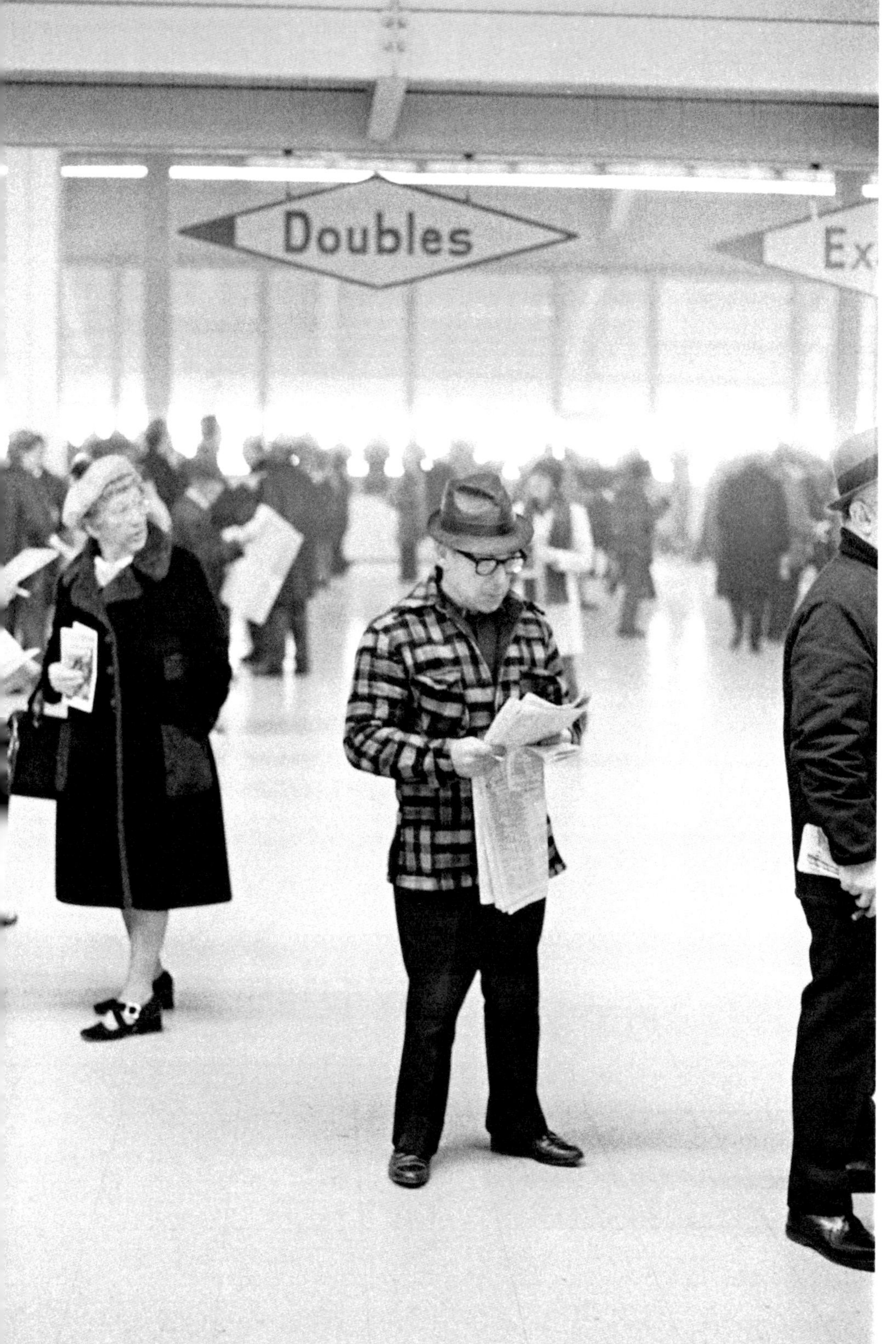

Doubles
Ex-

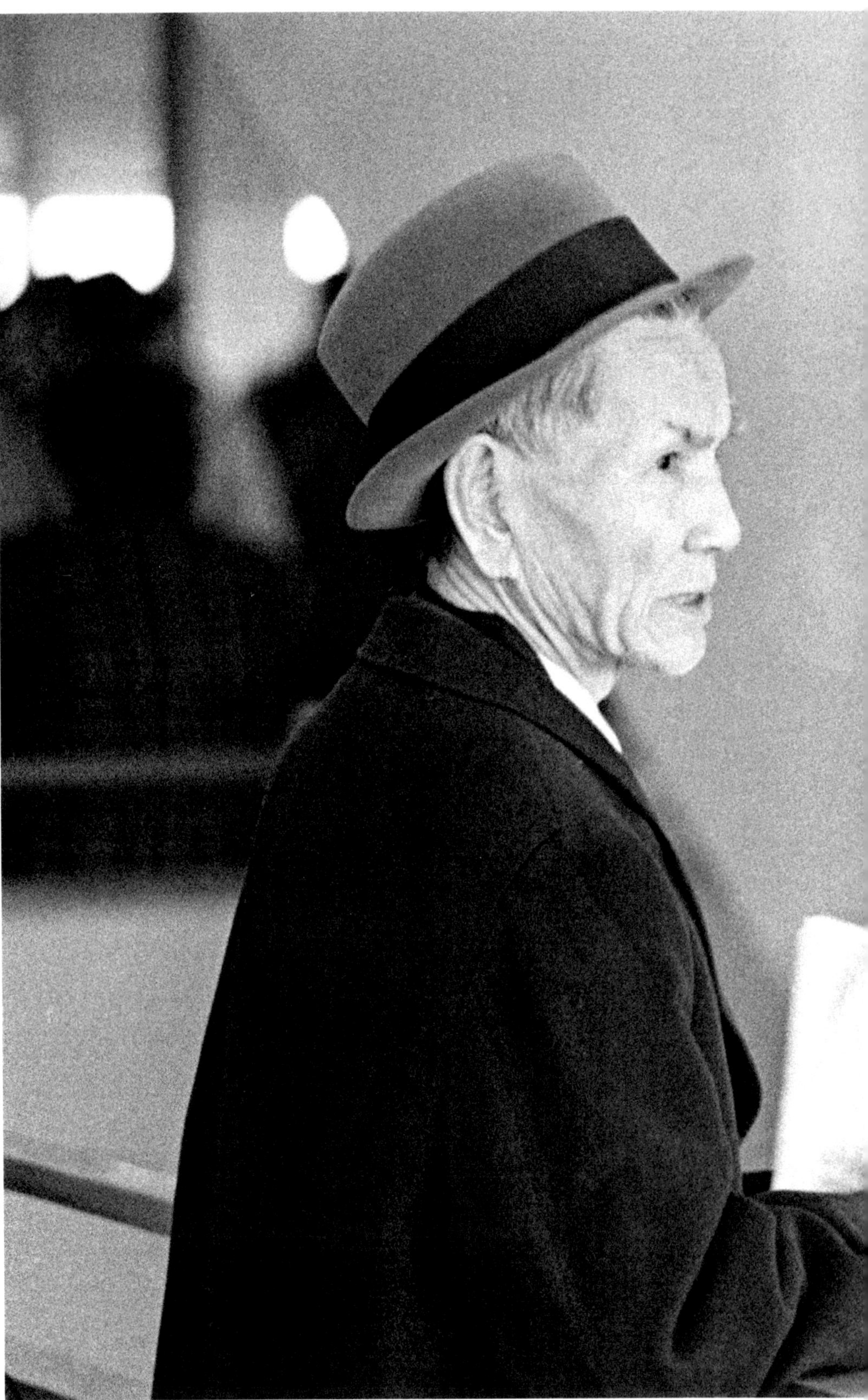

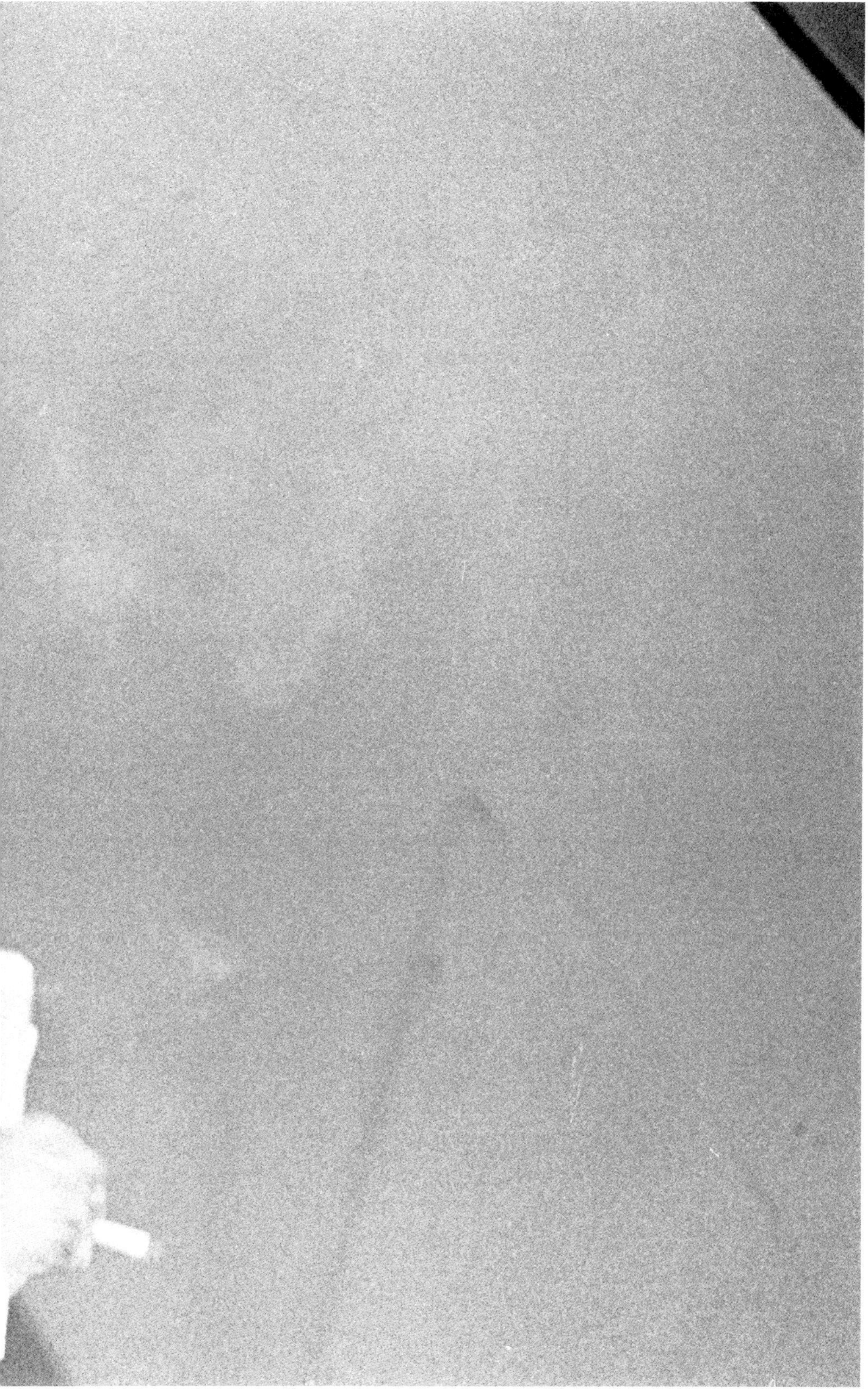

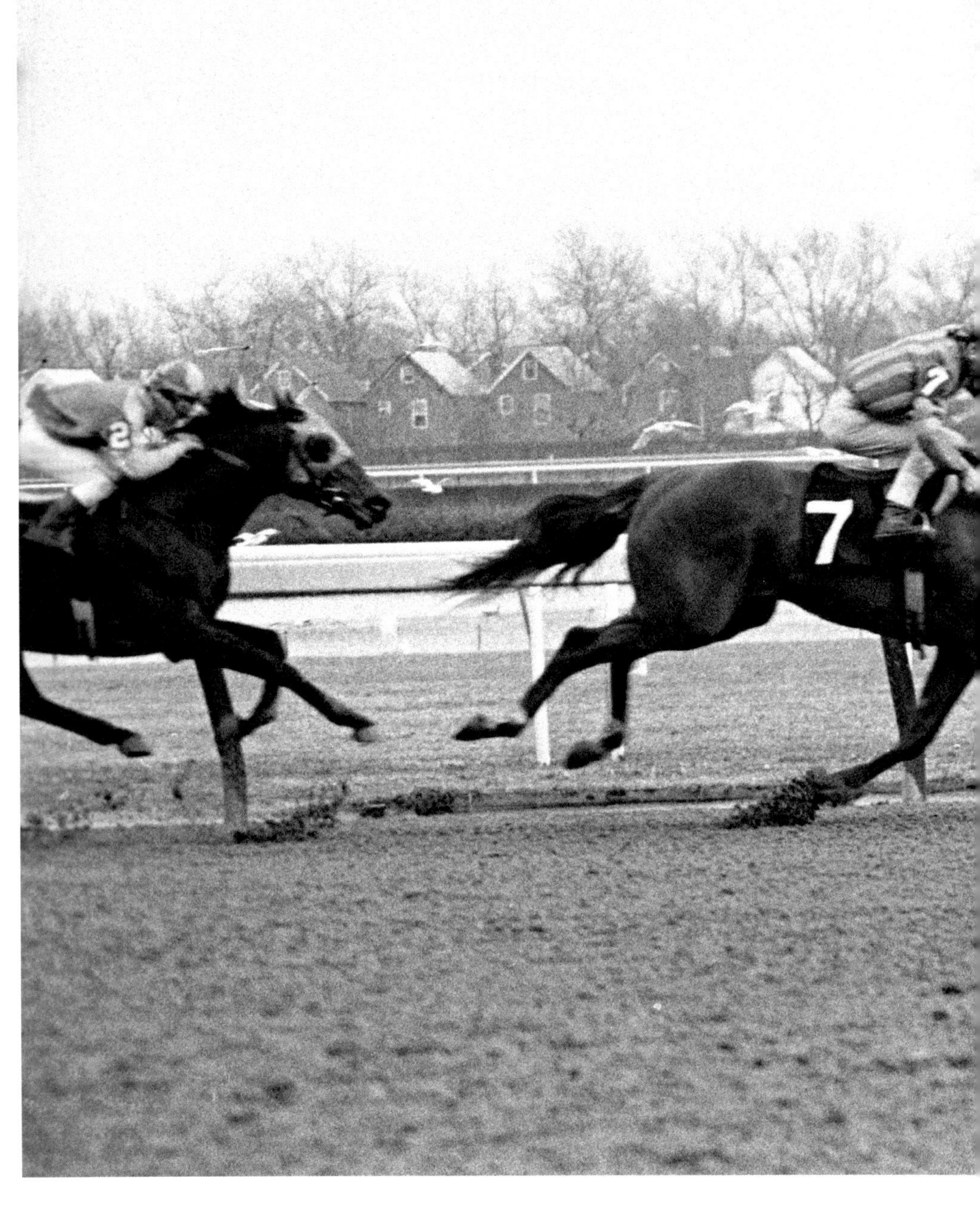

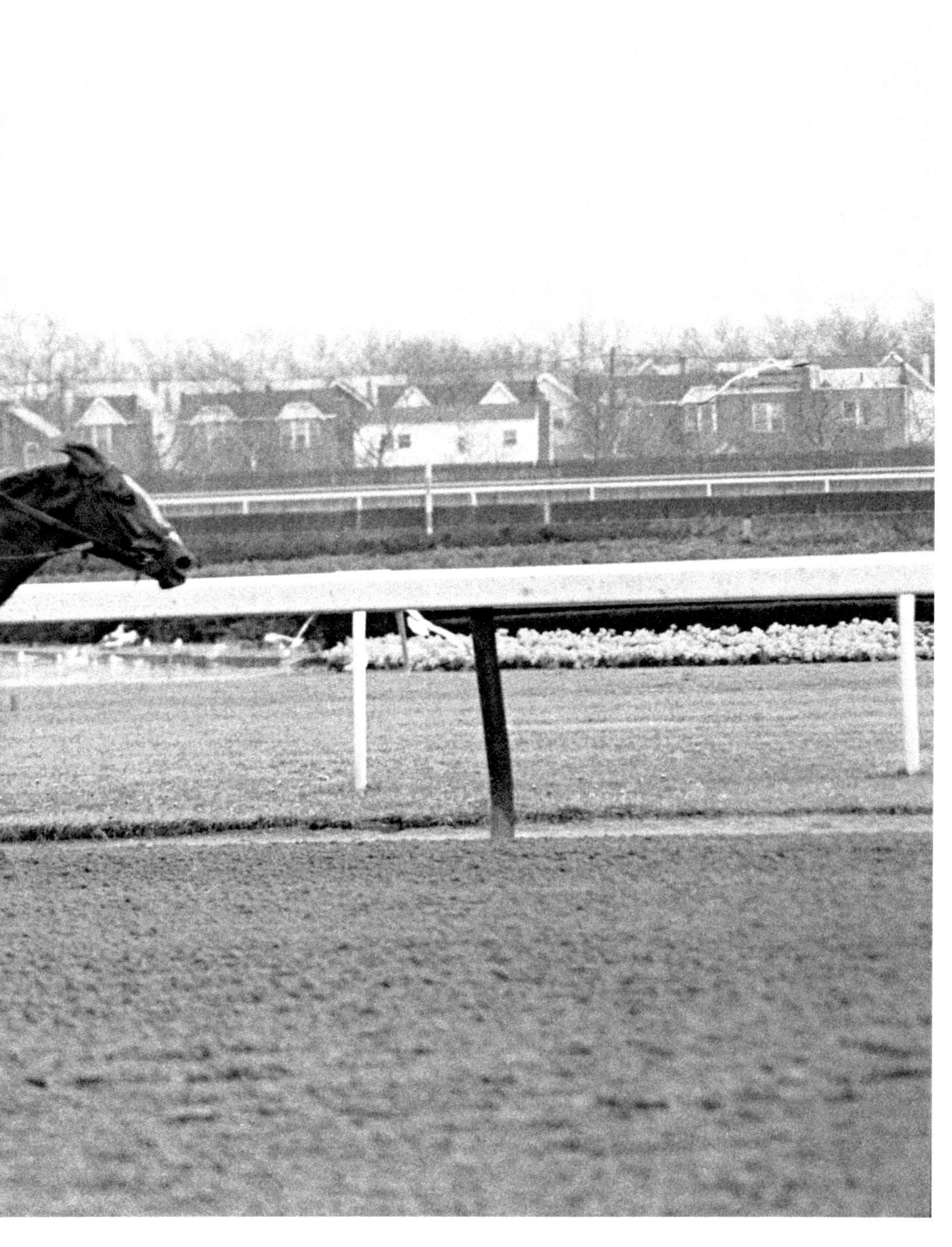

Before betting, handicappers would consider a horse's past performances, the day's weather, track conditions, the competing horses, and current betting odds in picking a winner. Win or lose, they repeated this process for every race throughout the day.

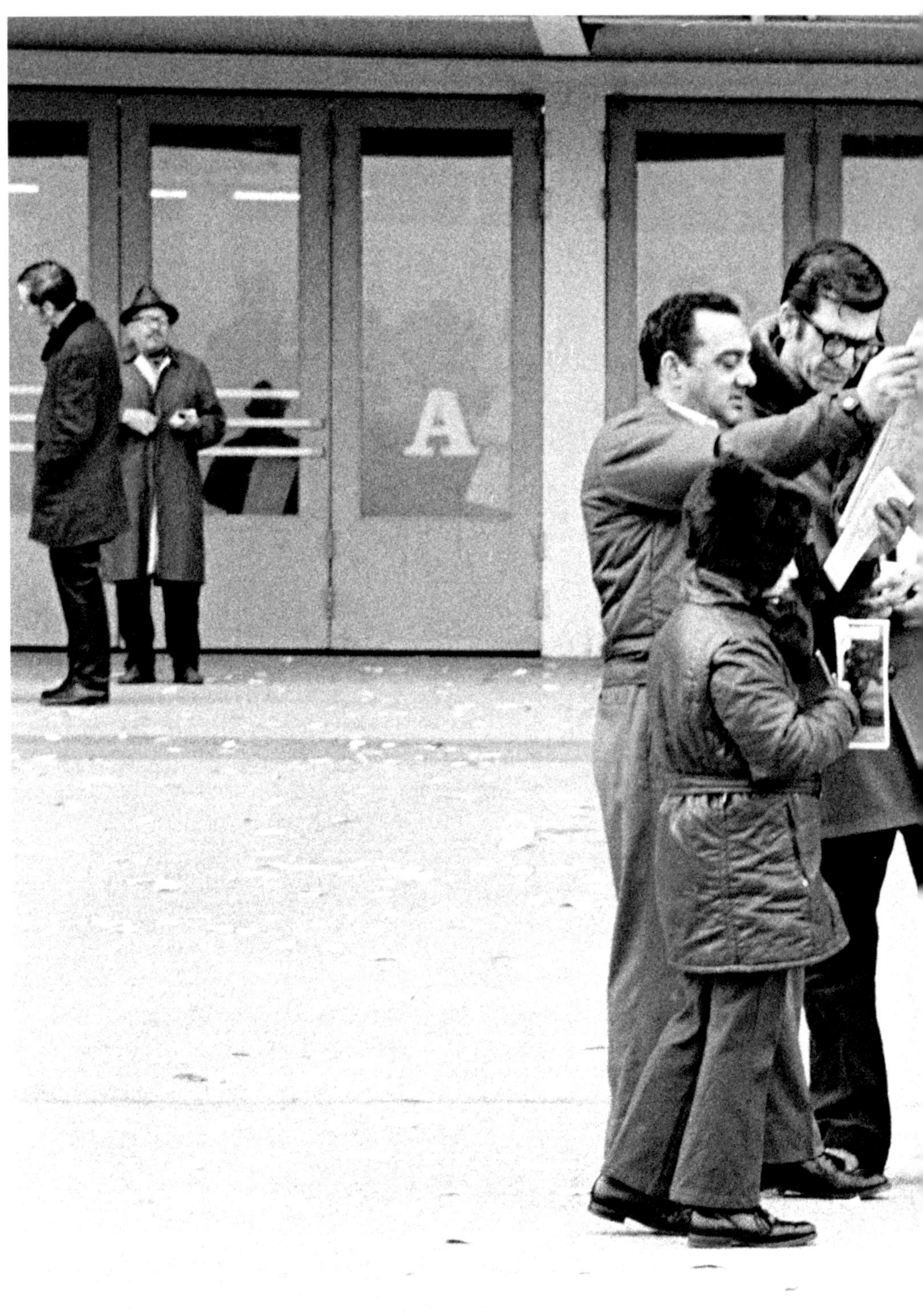

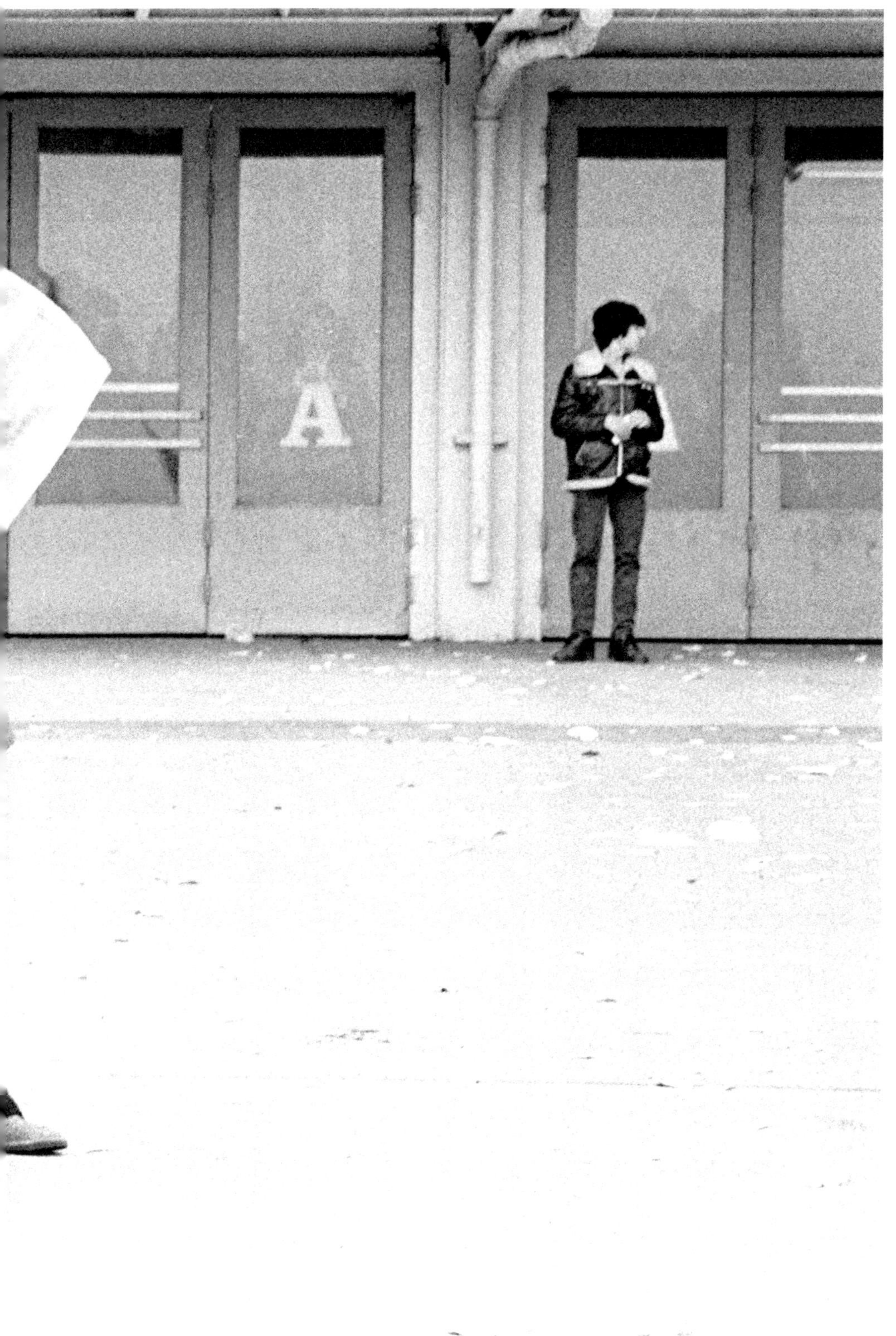

I photographed them as they struggled to hold open both the large pages of their newspapers and their programs at the same time. It did not look like they were having fun.

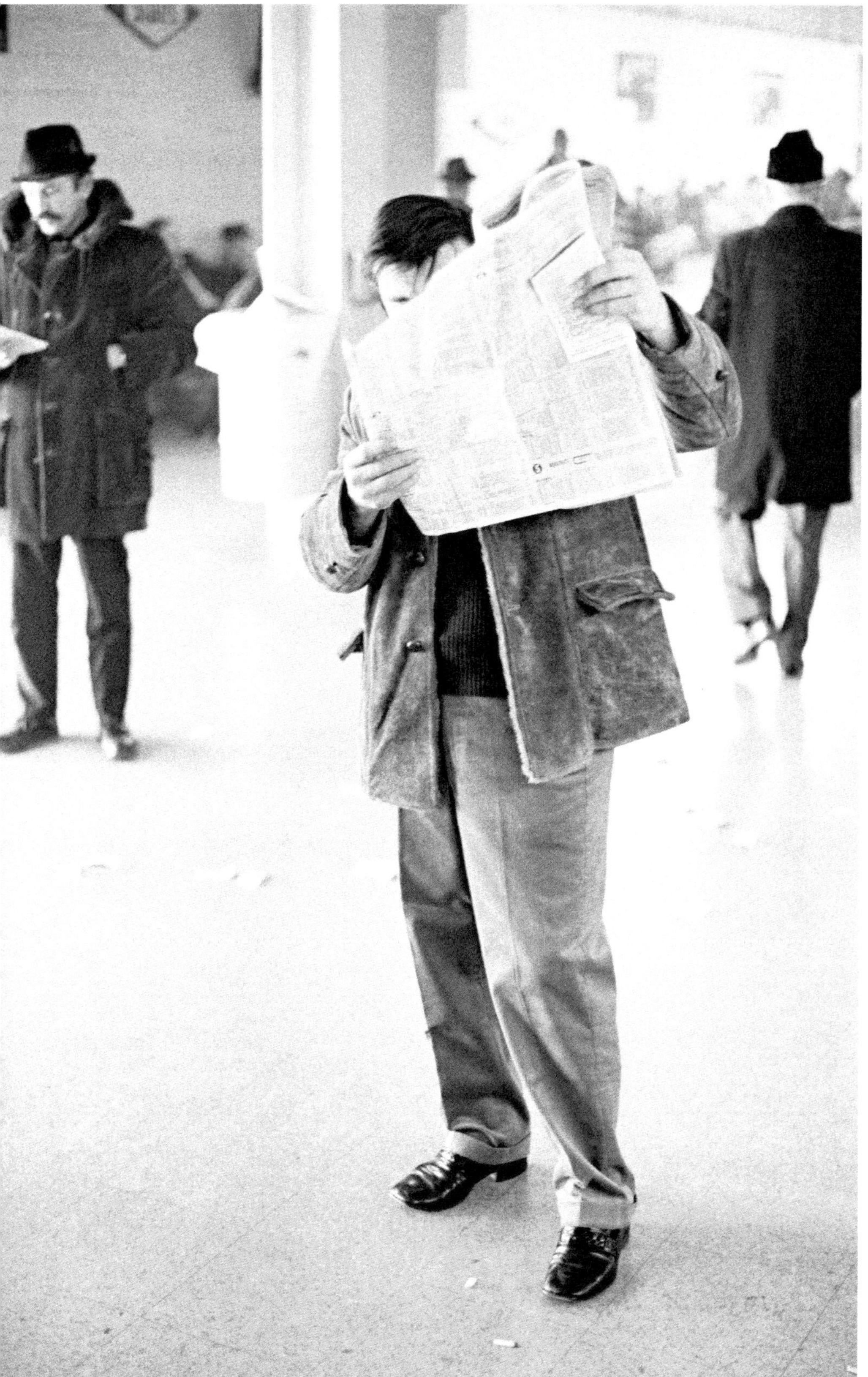

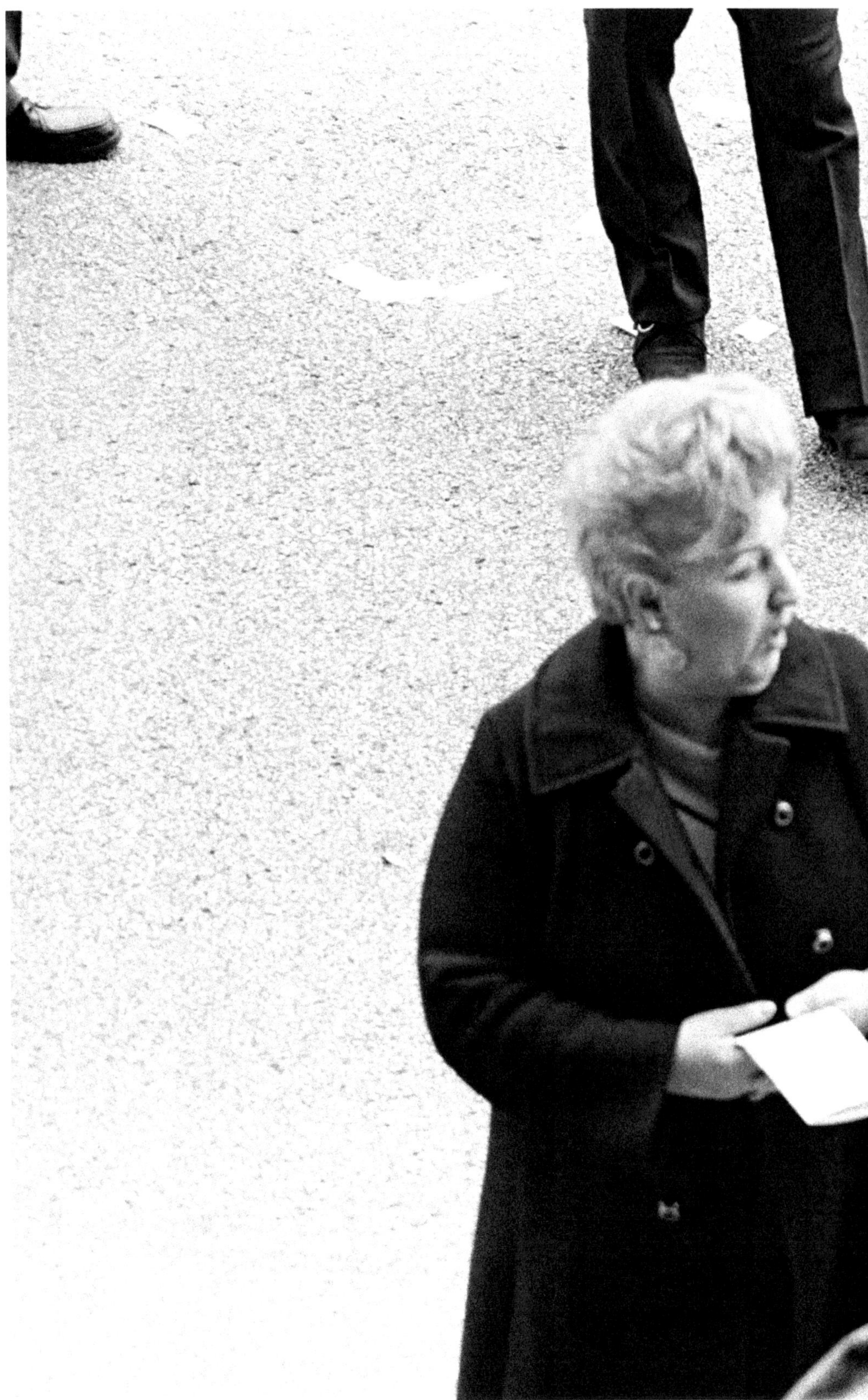

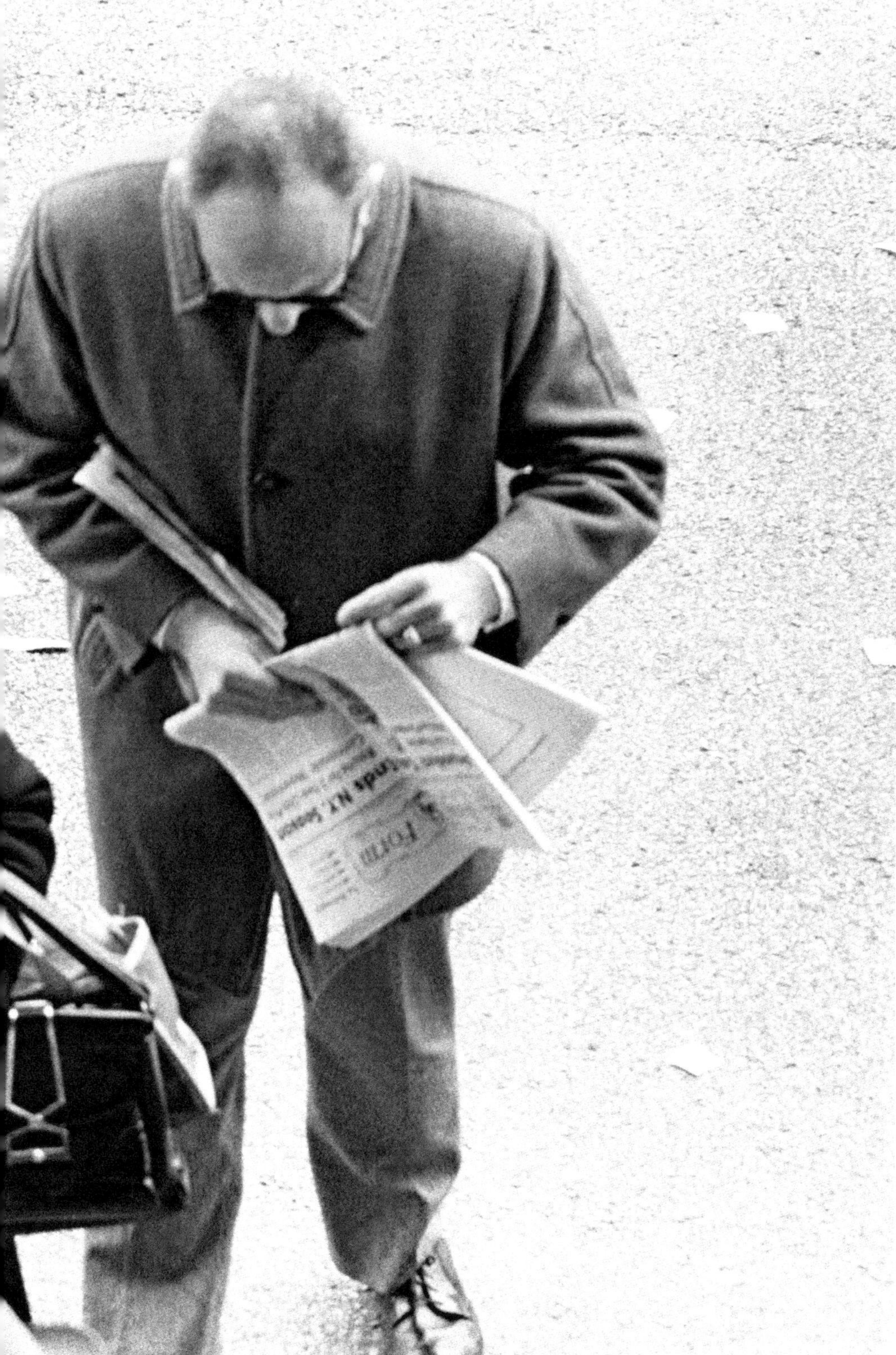

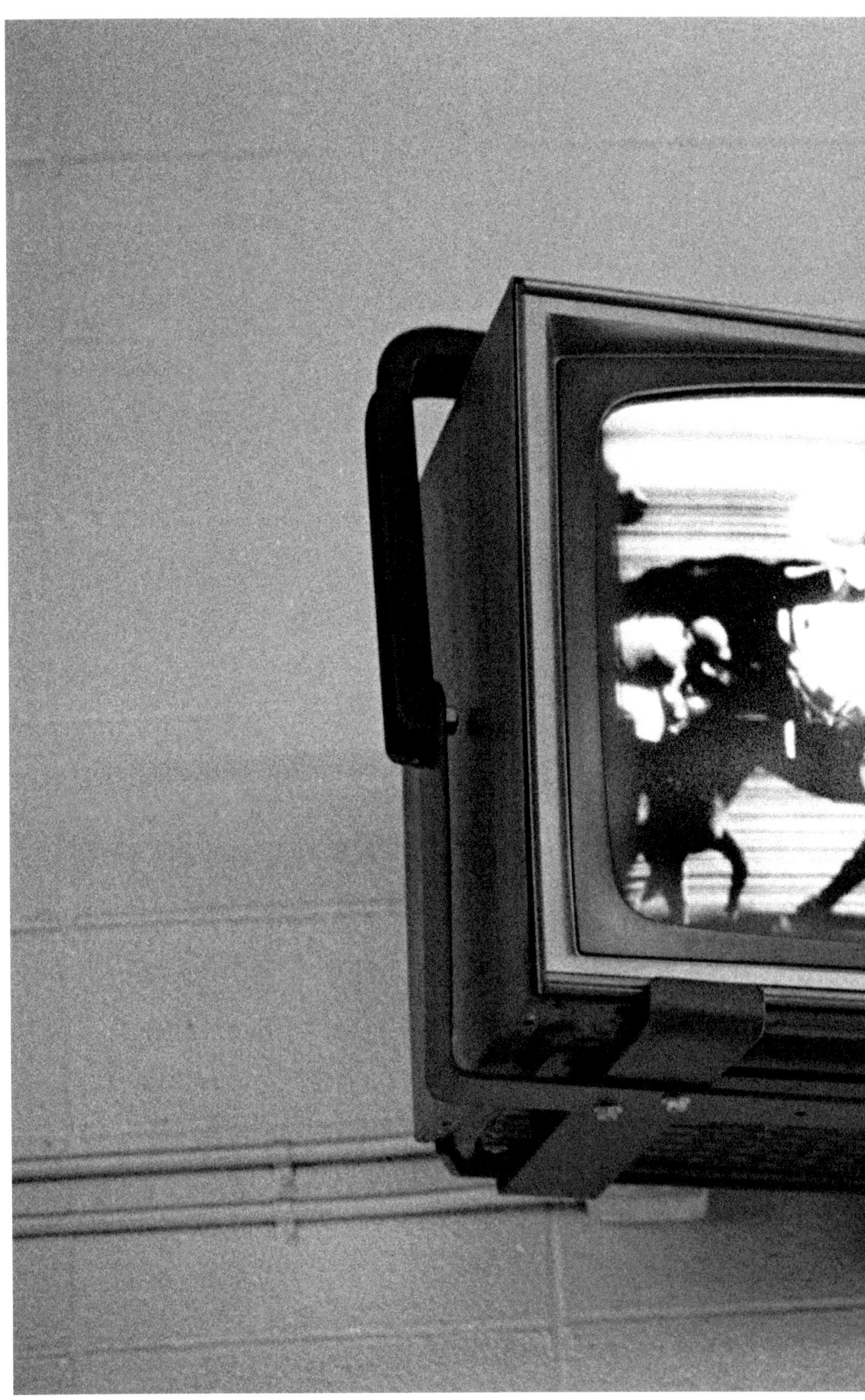

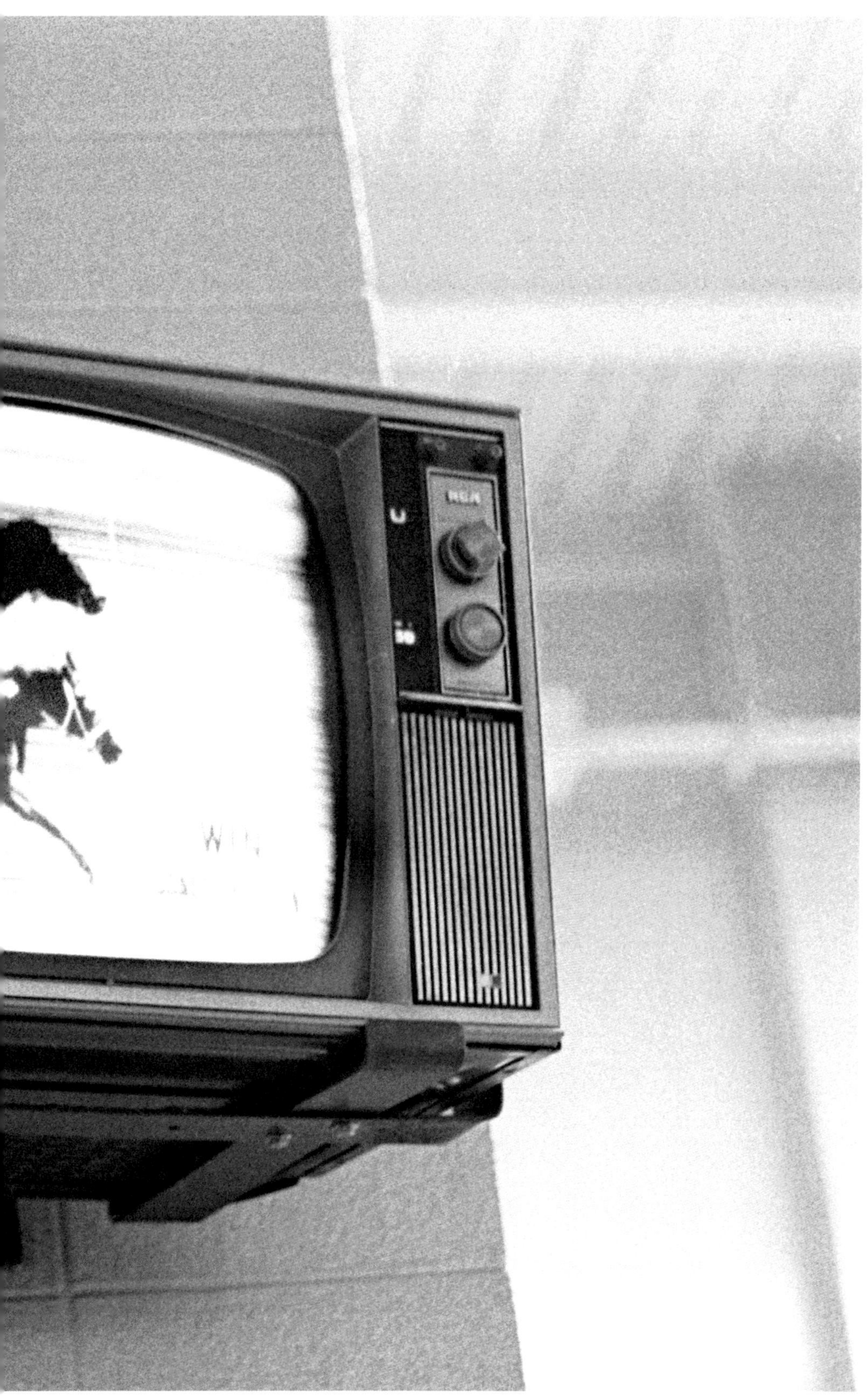

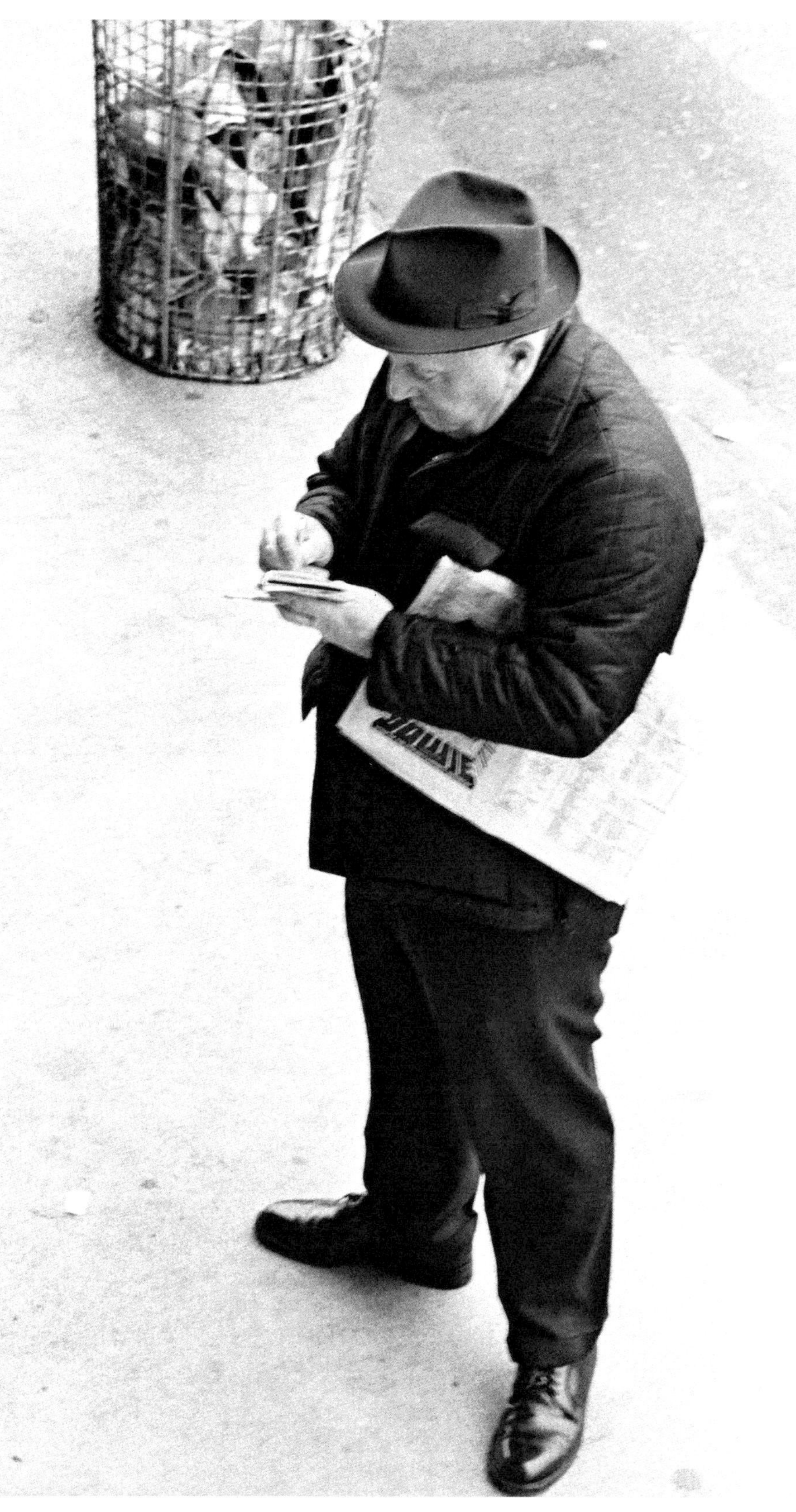

JOURNE

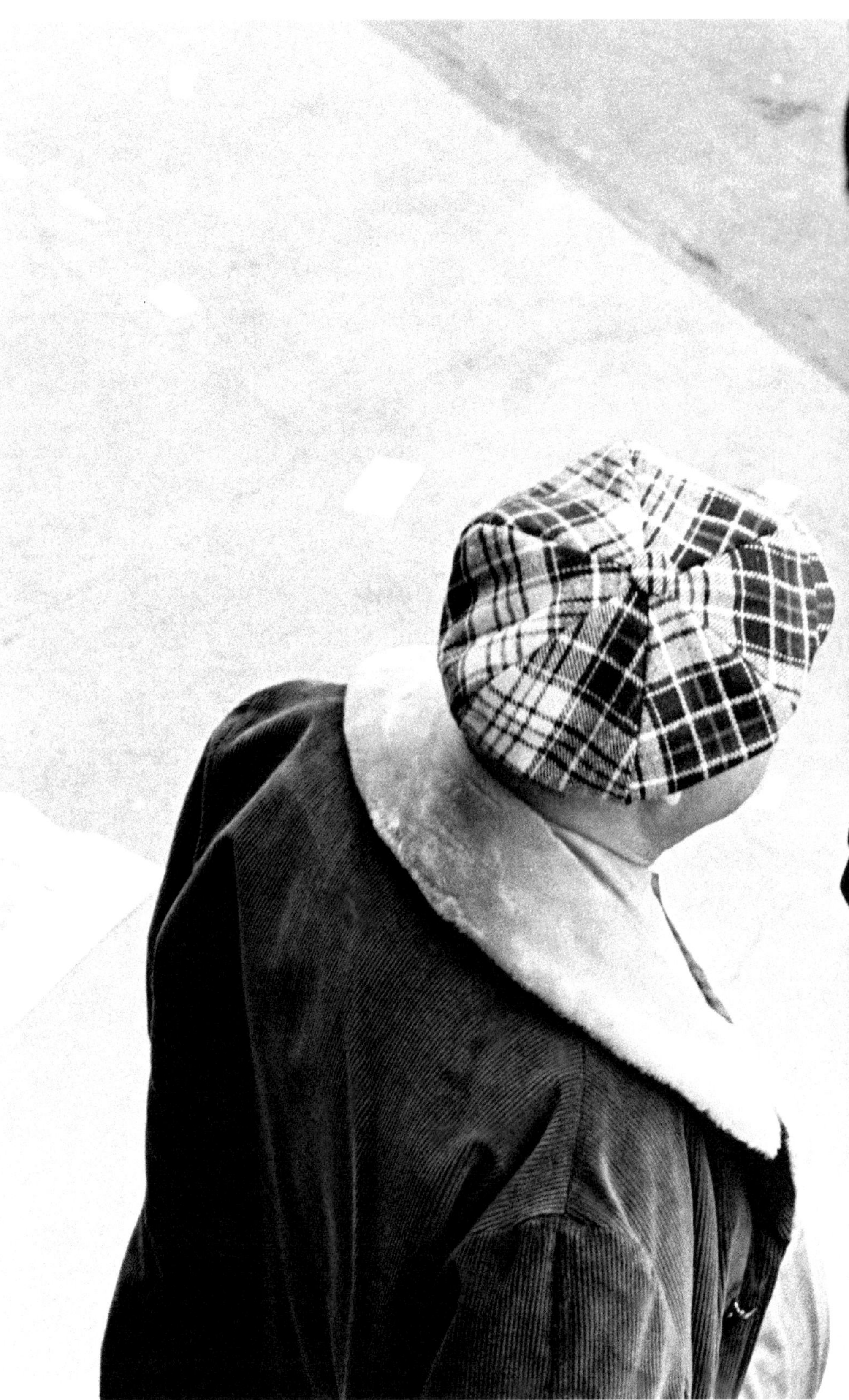

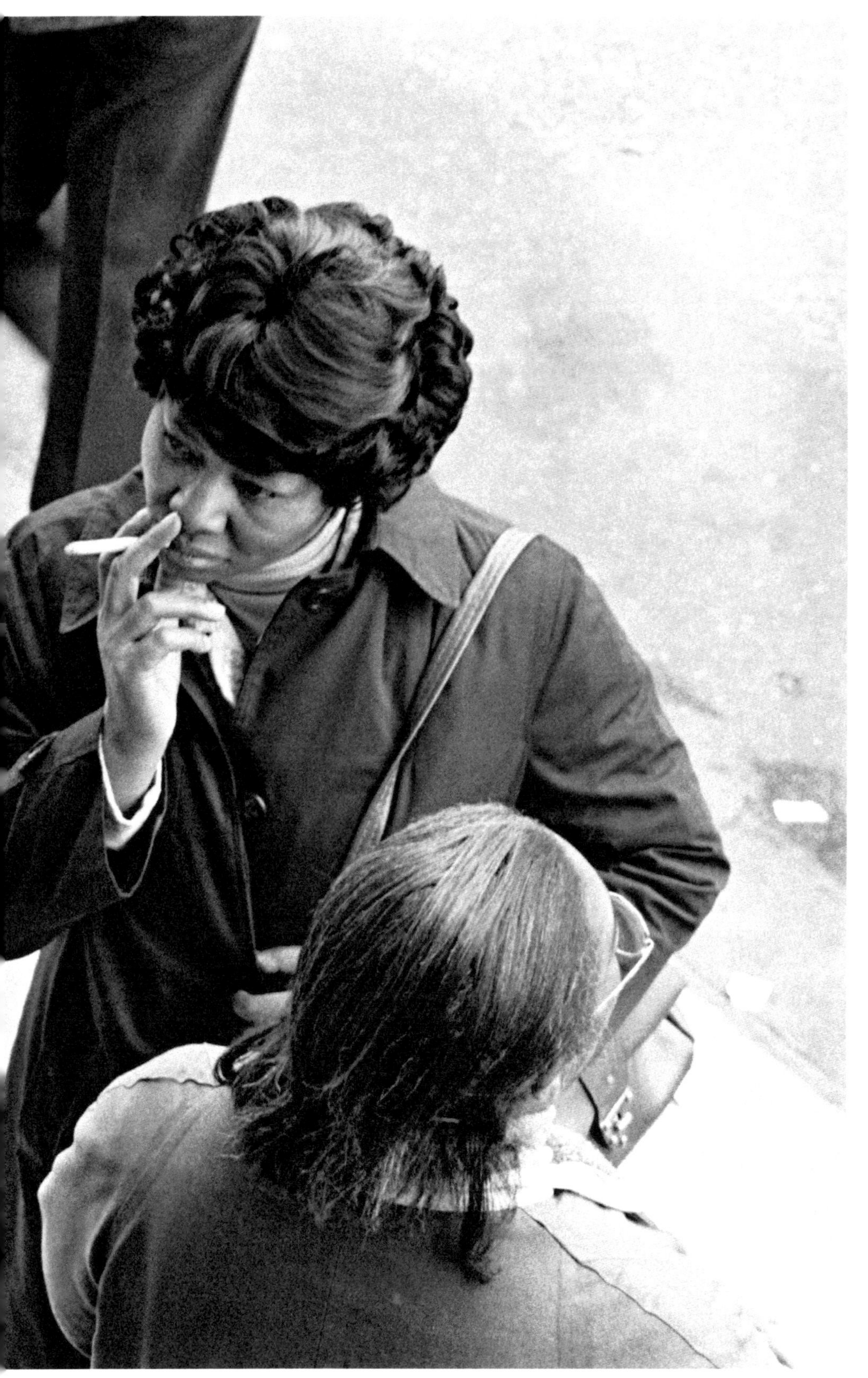

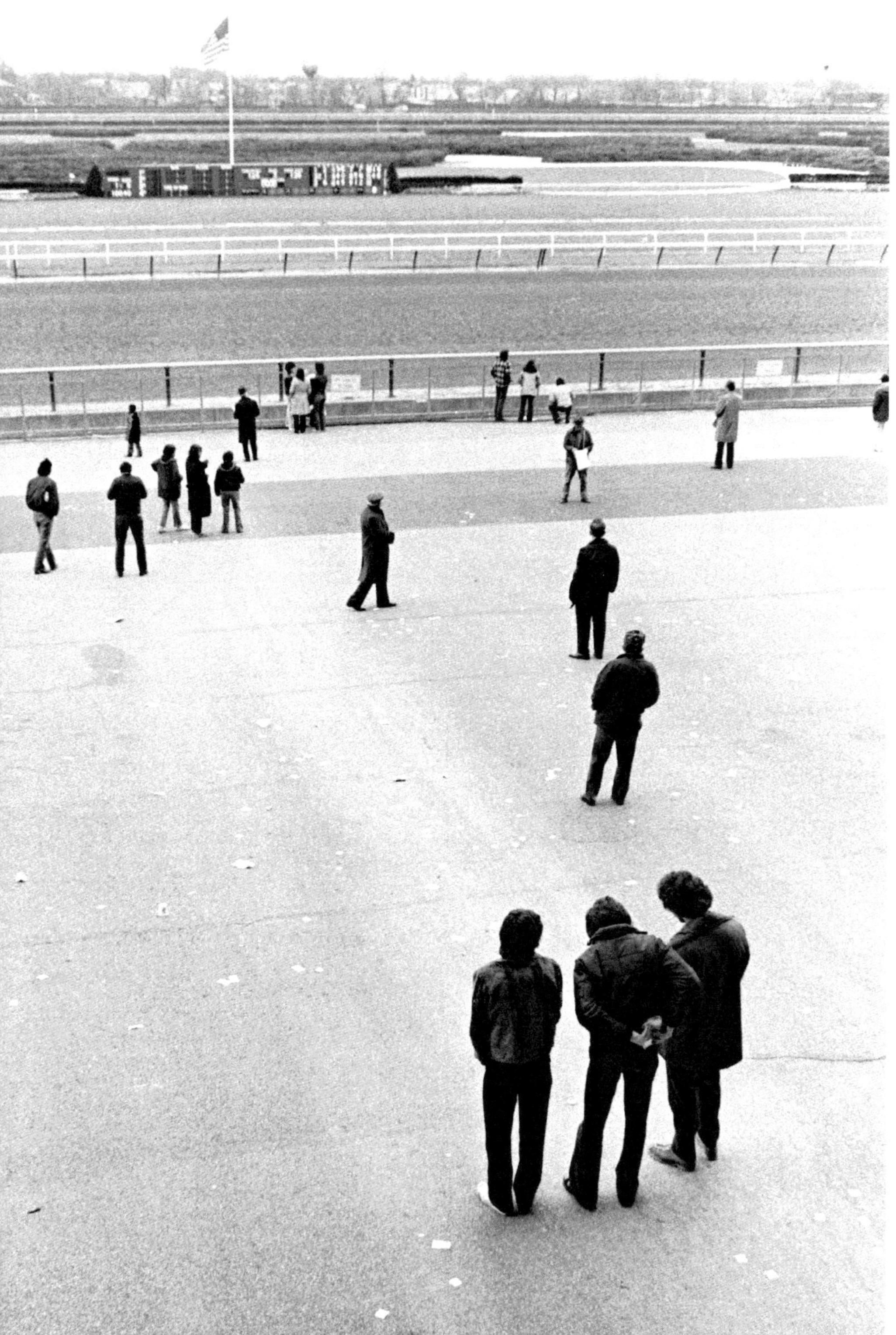

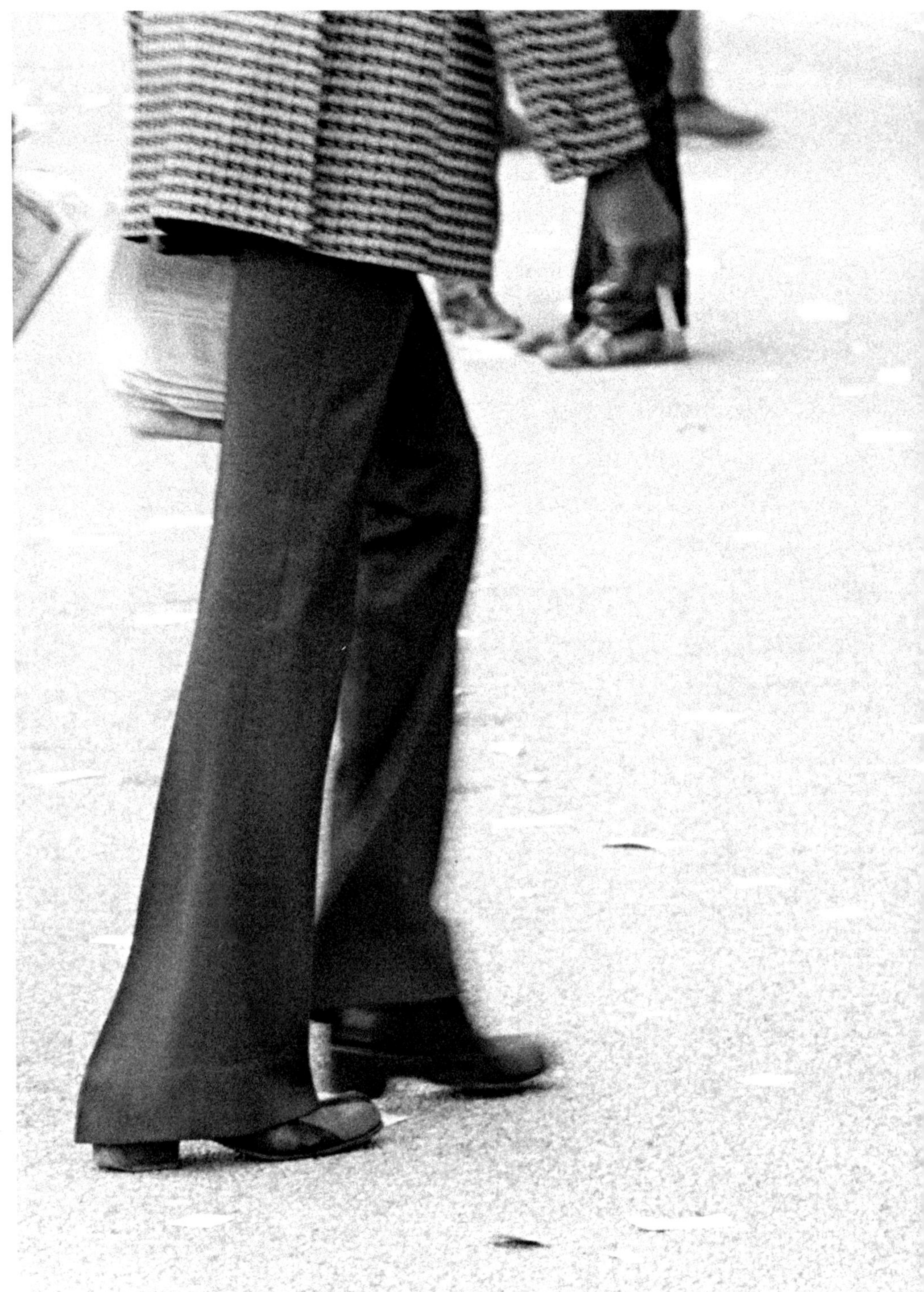

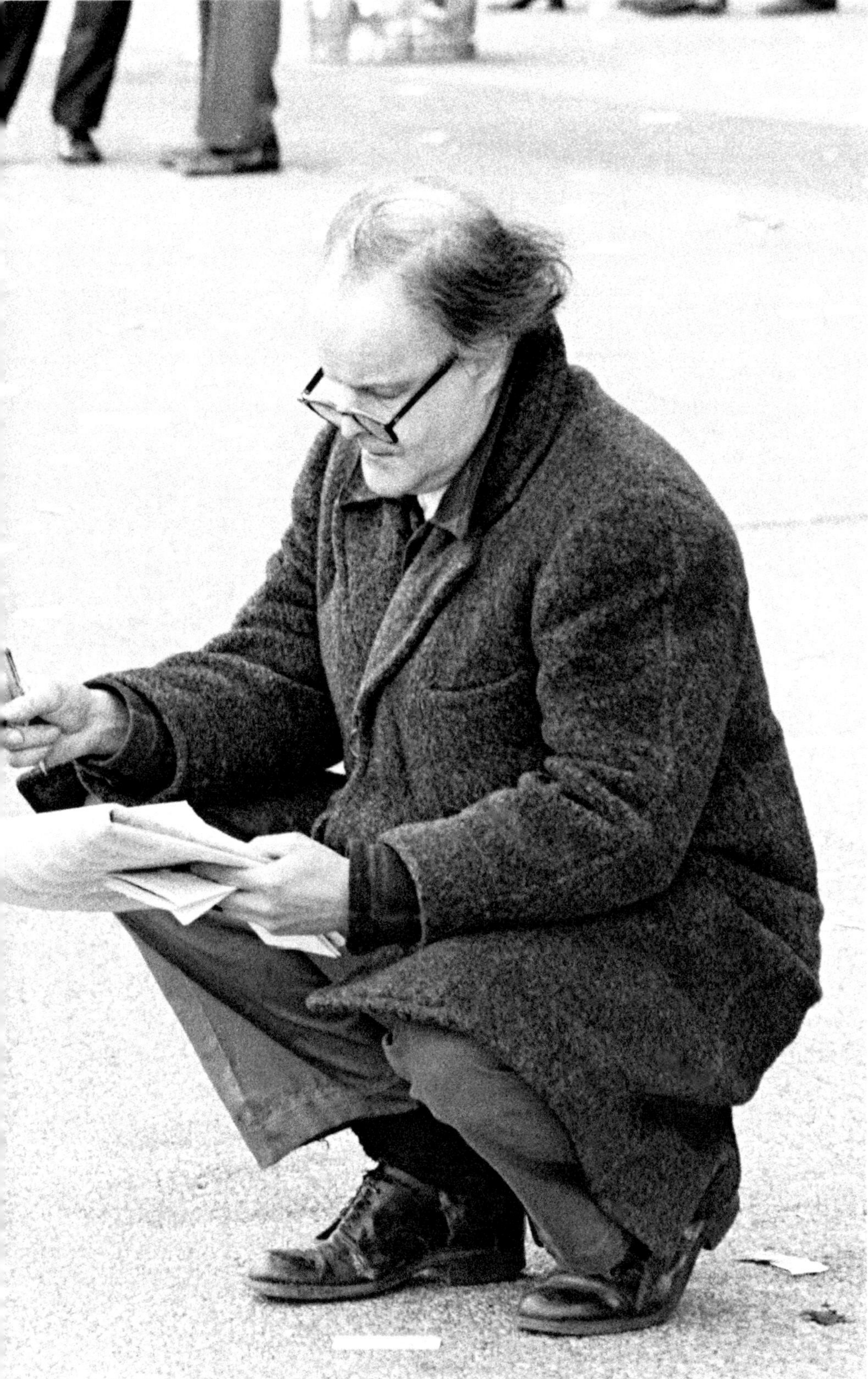

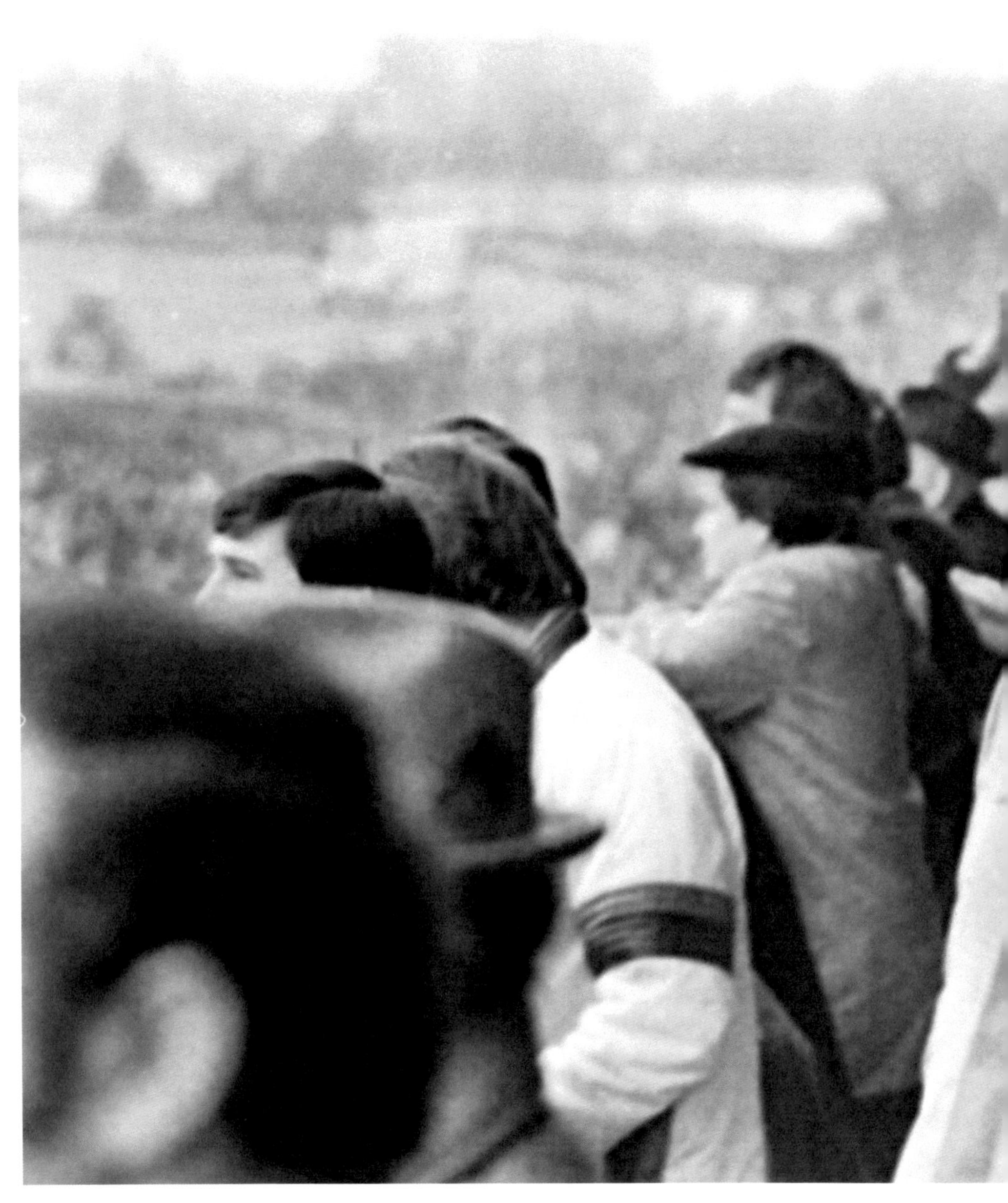

Much to the surprise of my father and uncle, I concocted
a system at Aqueduct. By betting on the favorite to place
"finish third" and a long shot to win, I won $200.

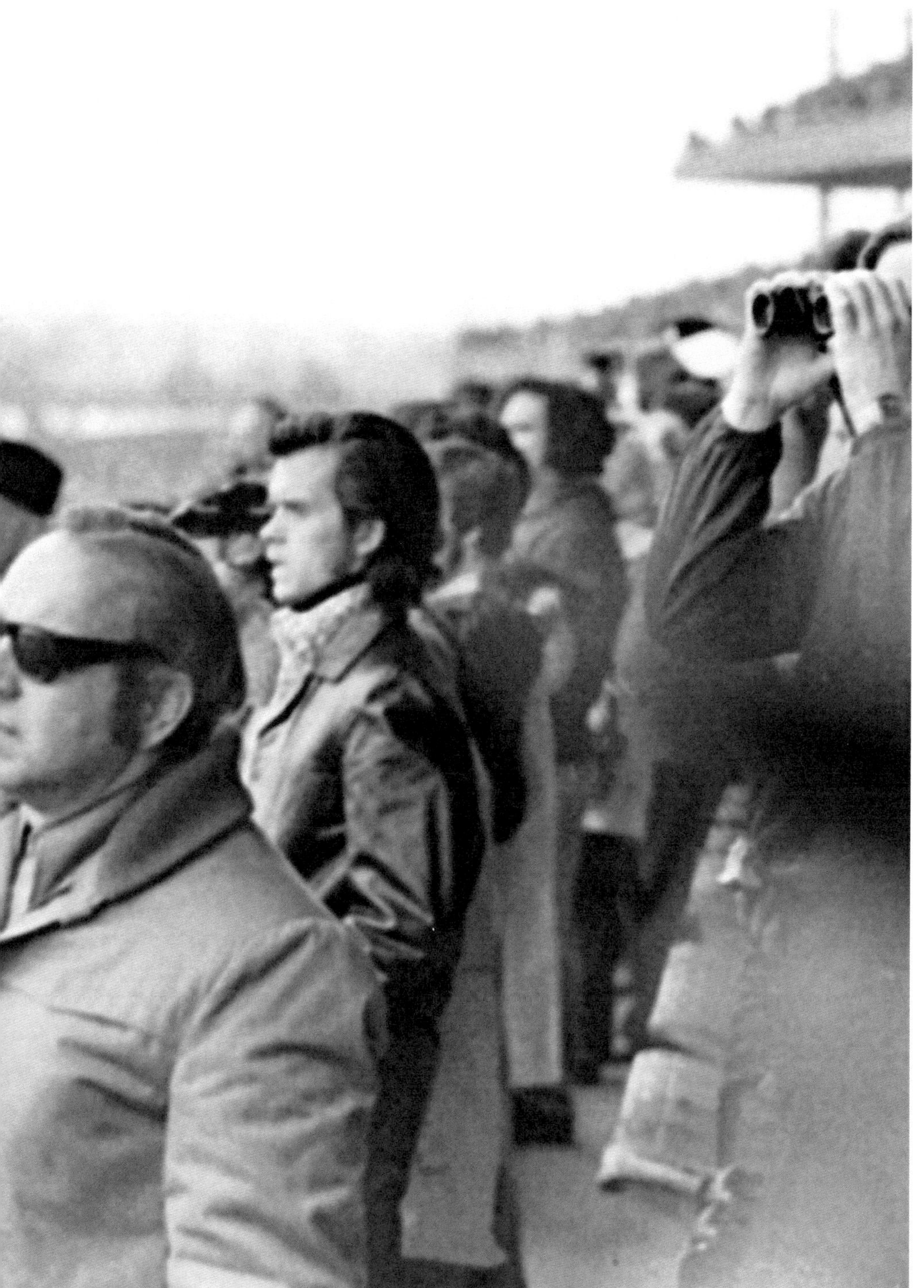

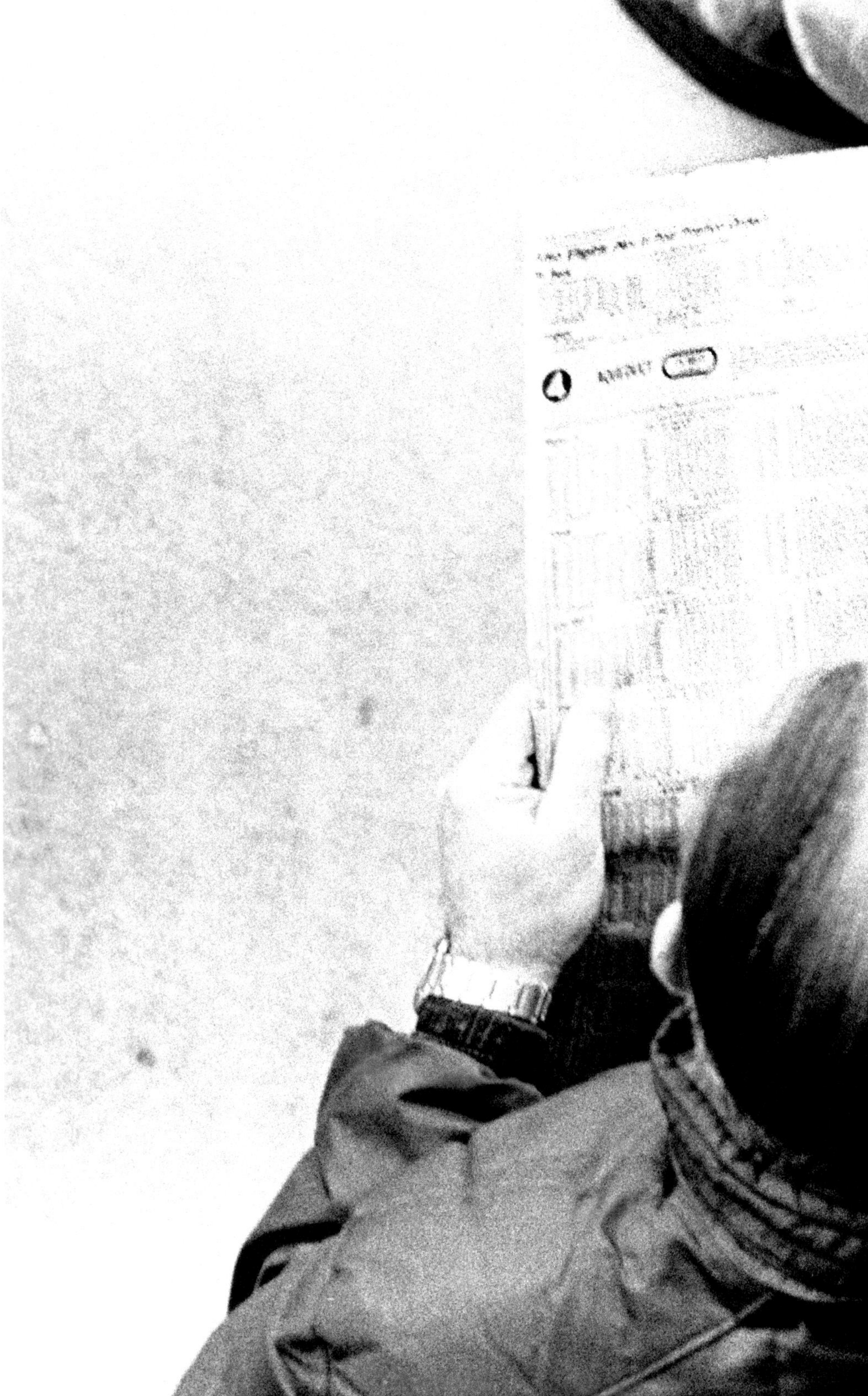

However, my system did not stand the test of time.
My father and I returned to Aqueduct a few days later.
I lost half my winnings and have never gone back.

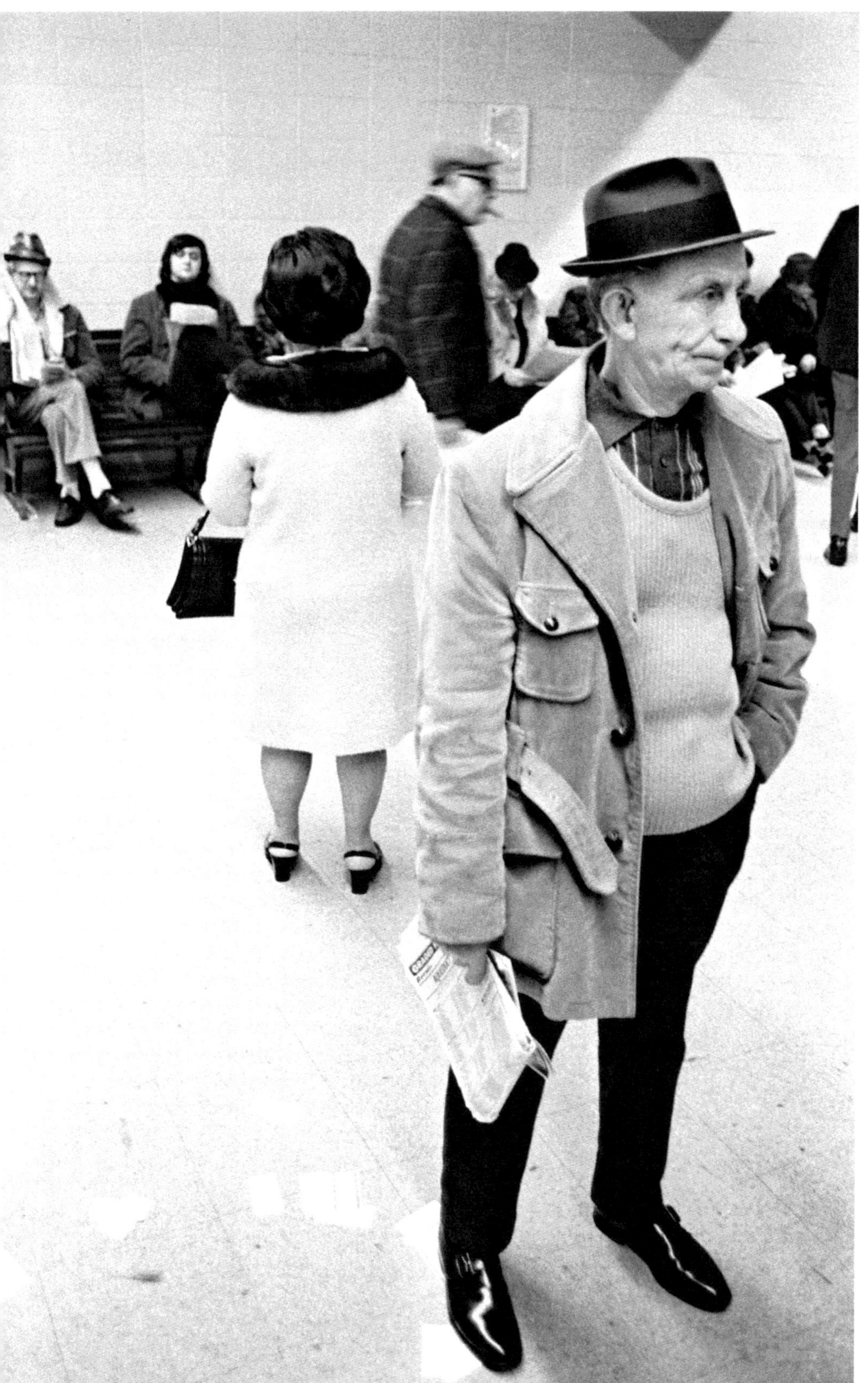

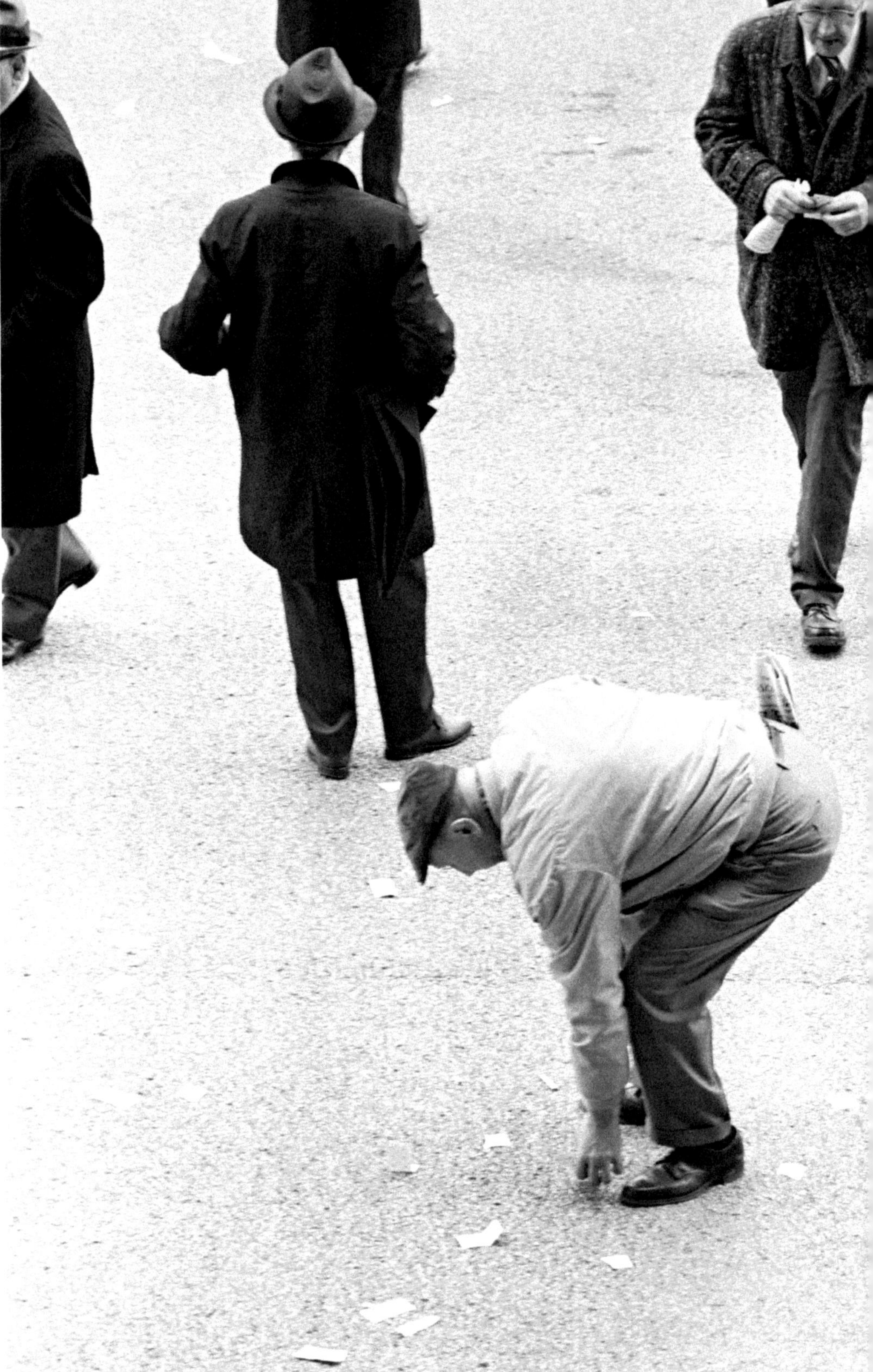

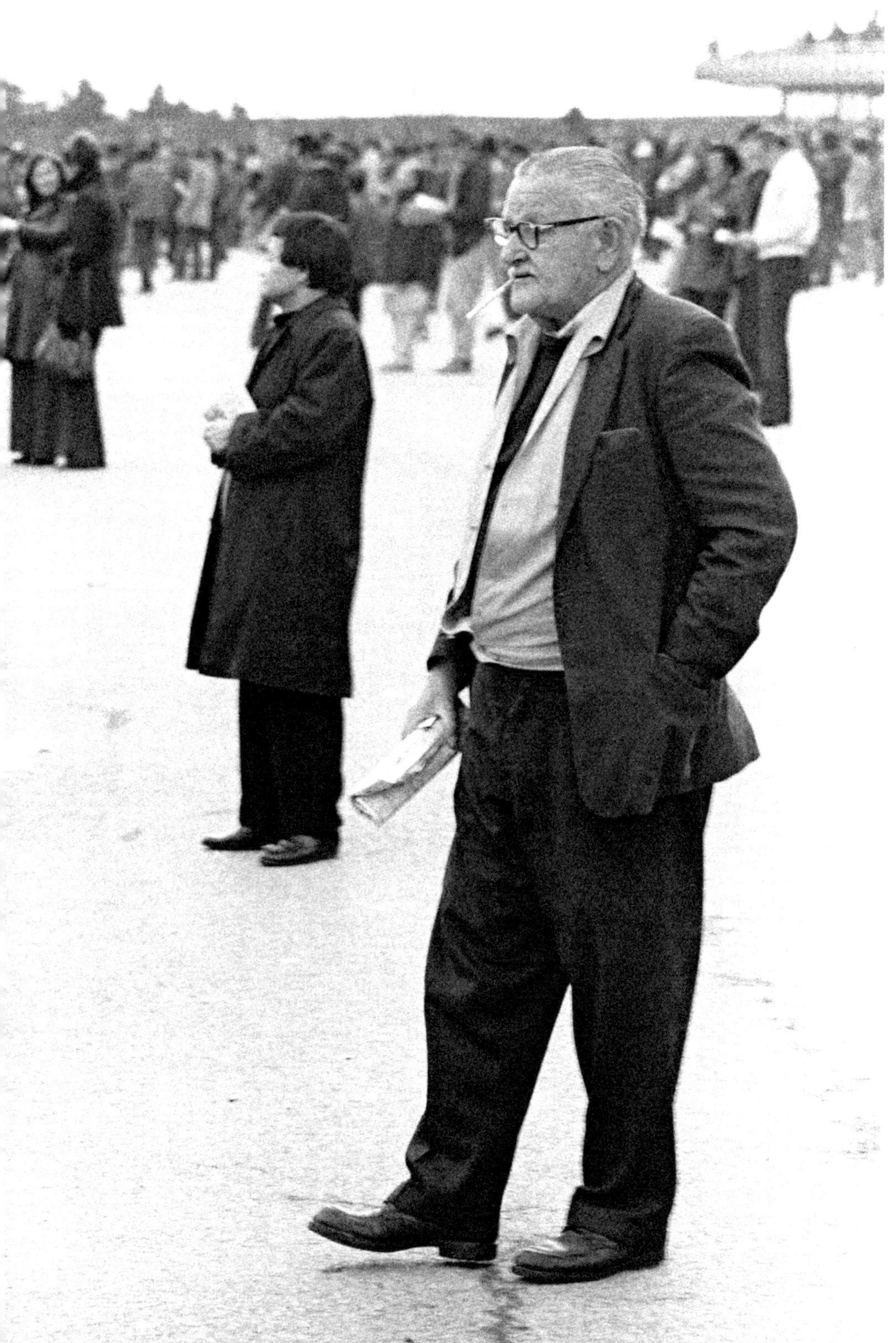

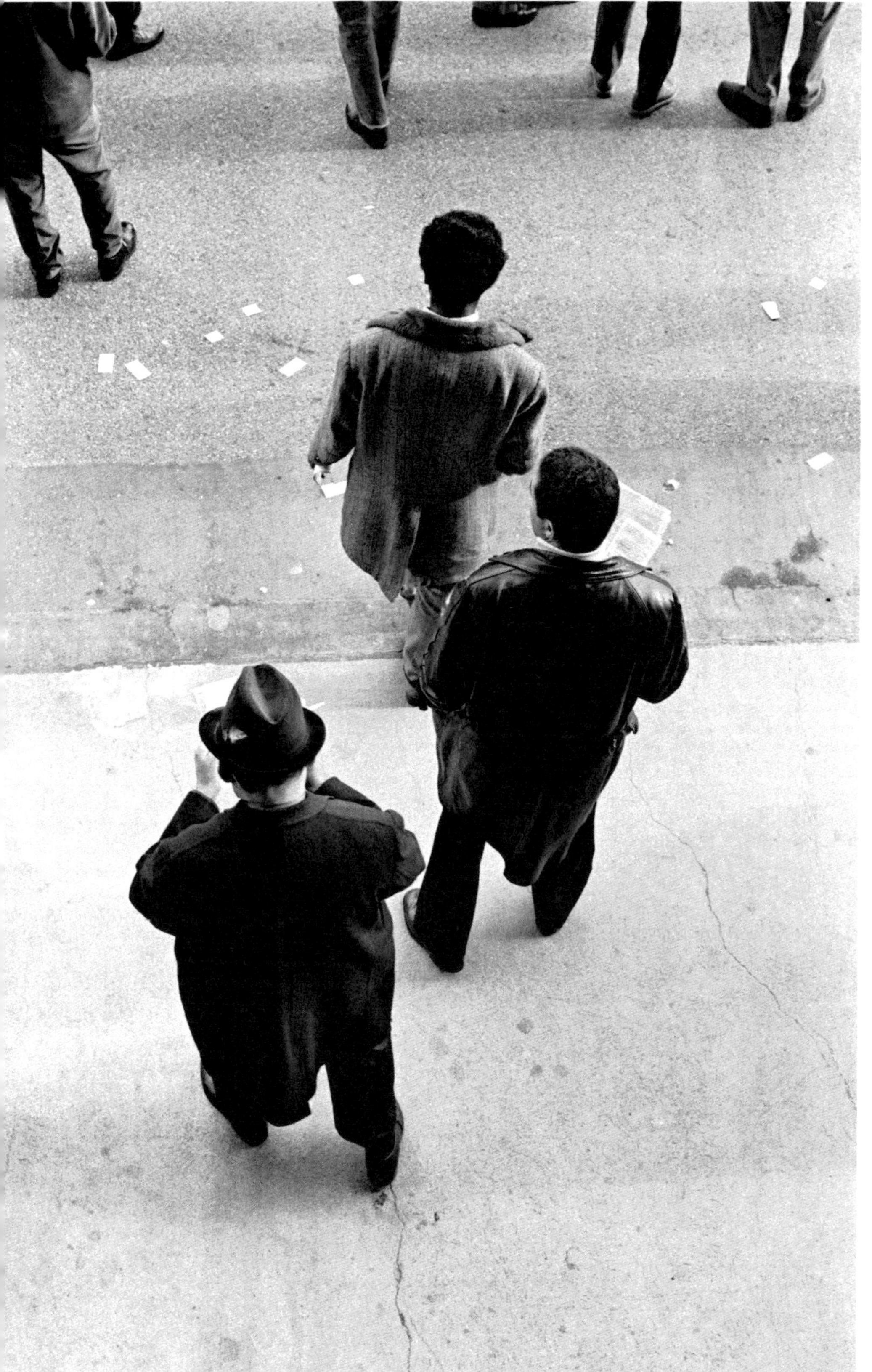

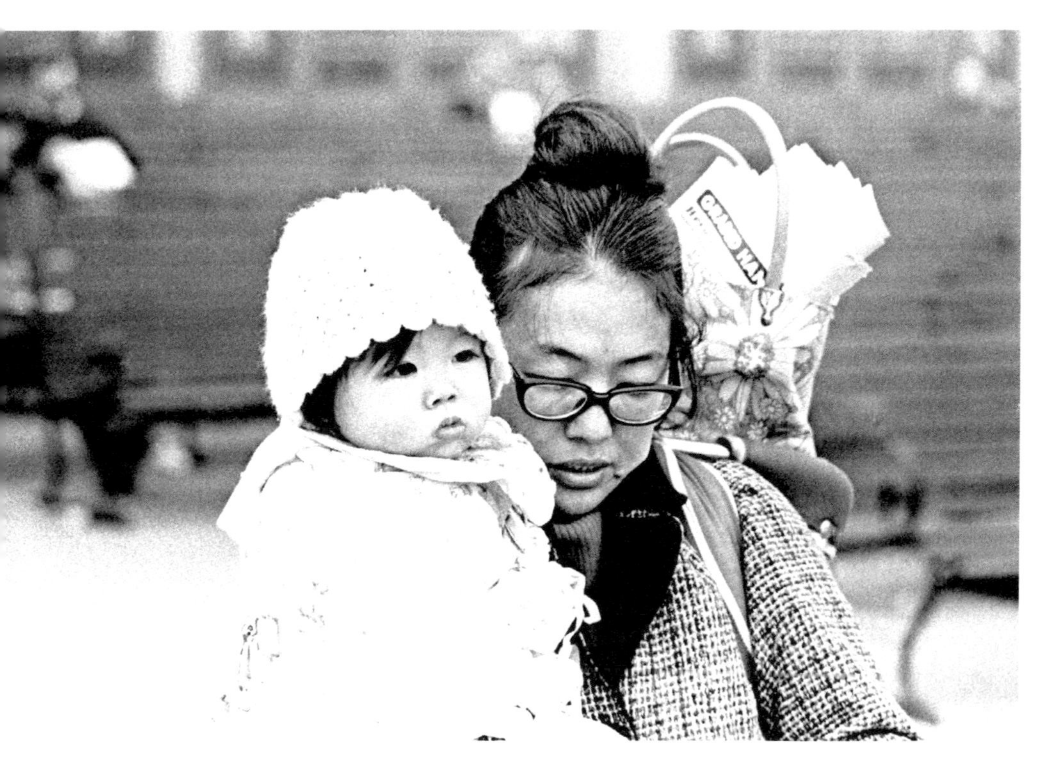

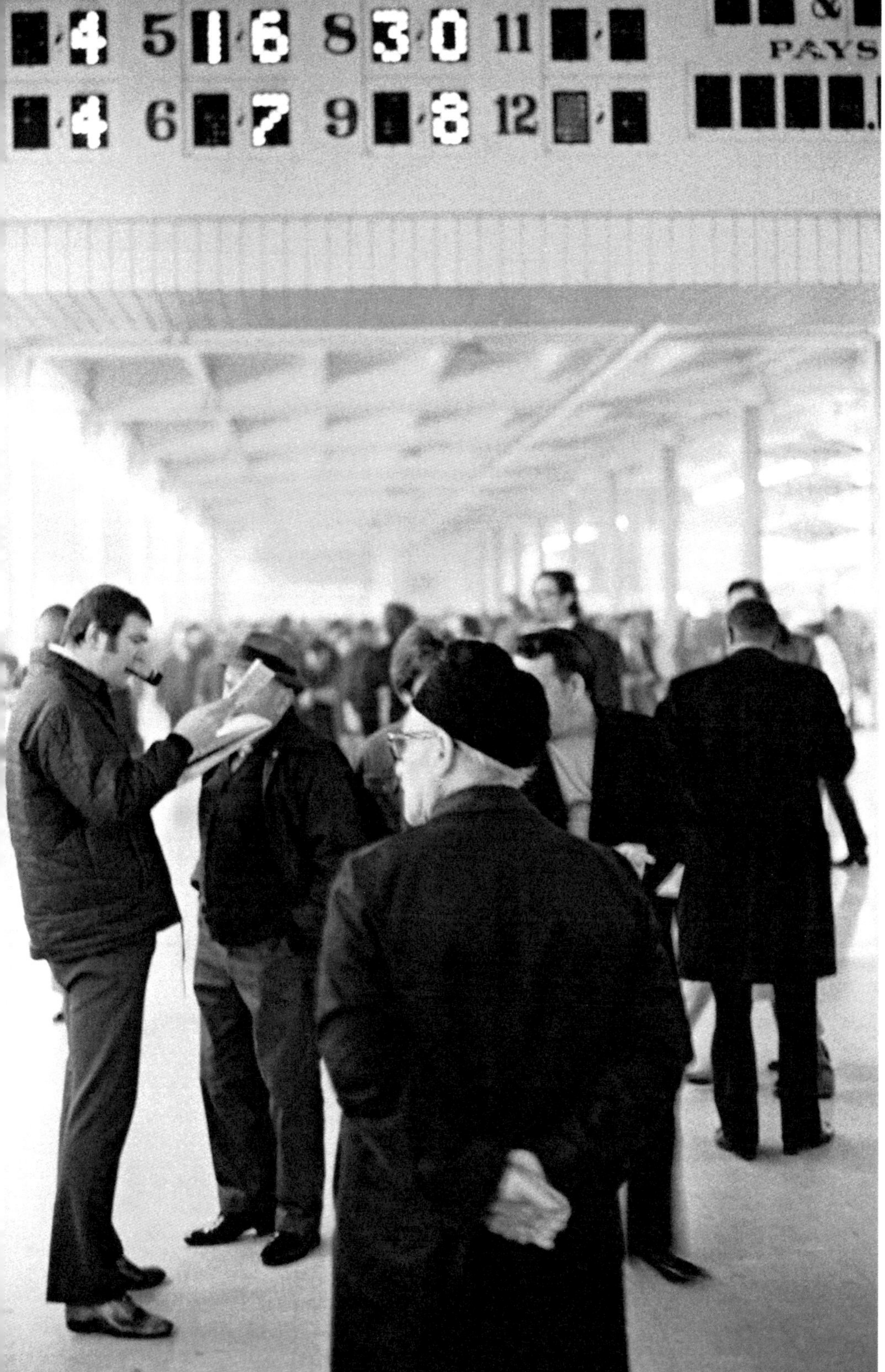
4 5 6 8 30 11
4 6 7 9 8 12
&
PAYS

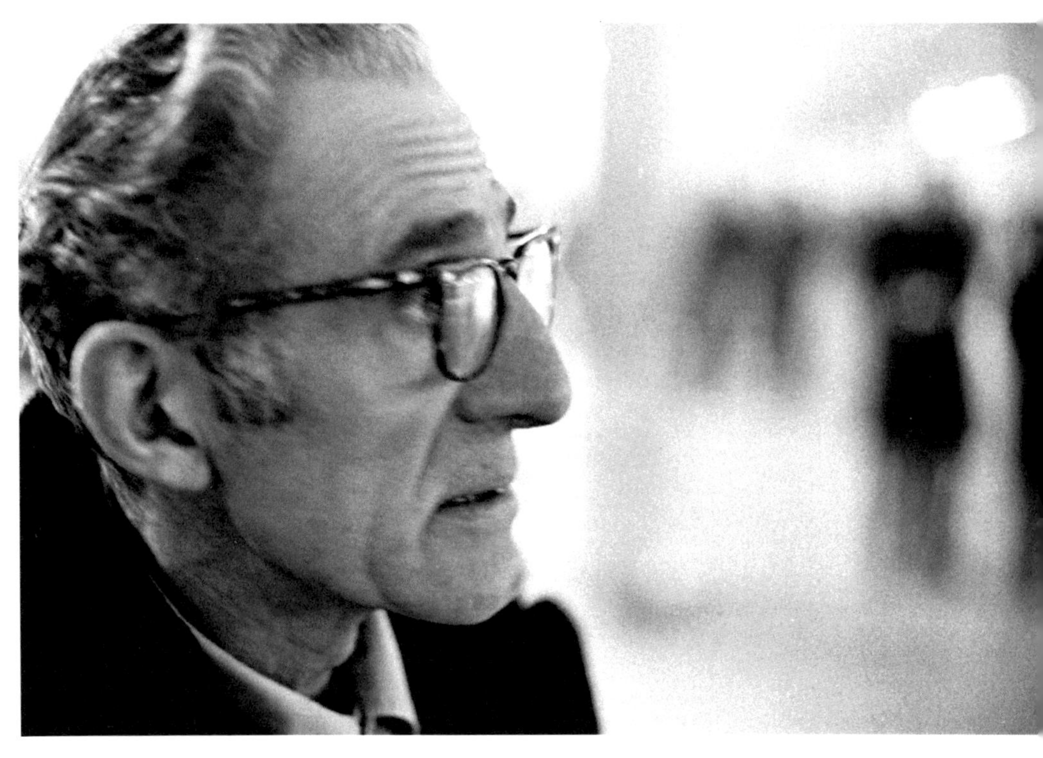

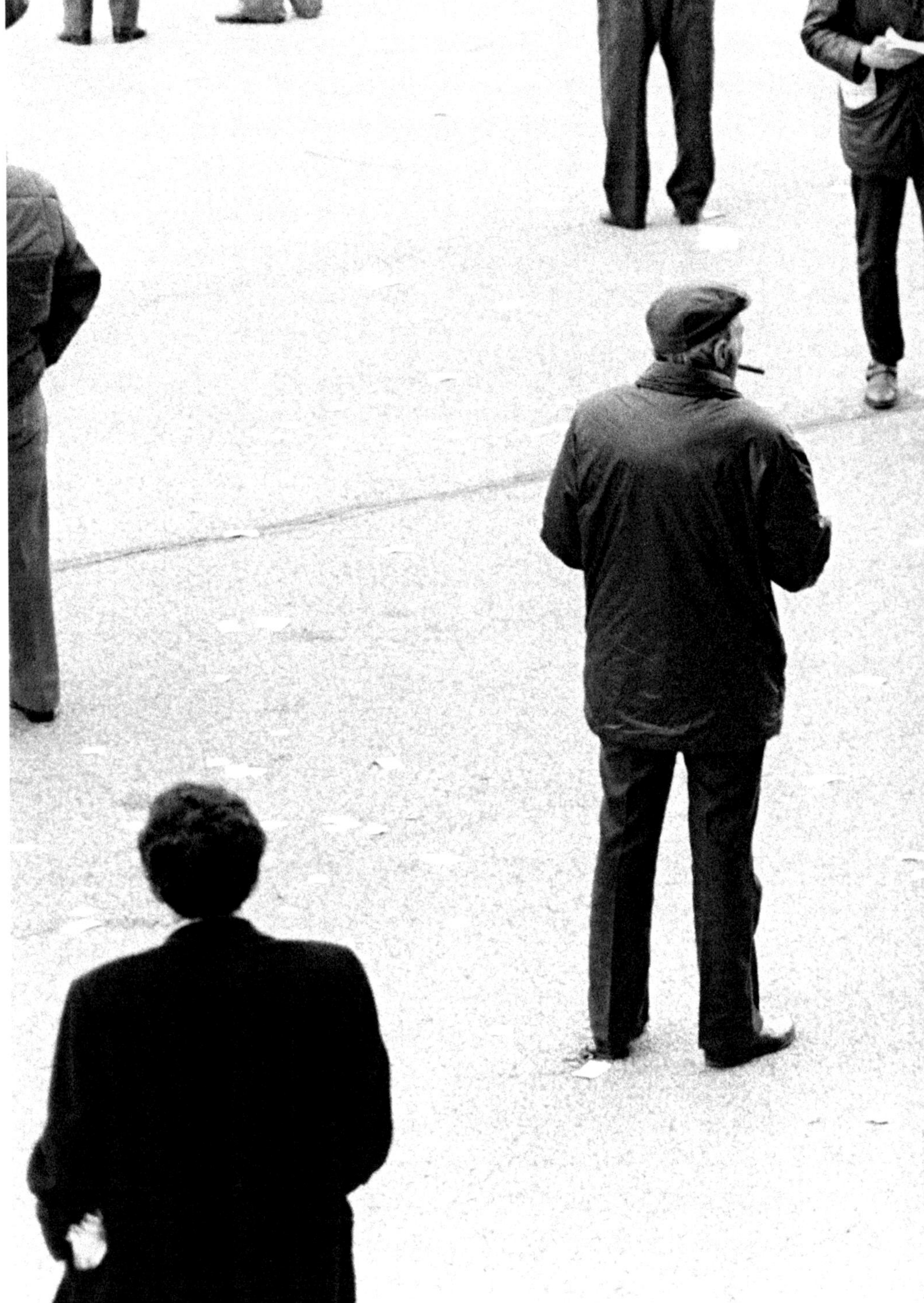

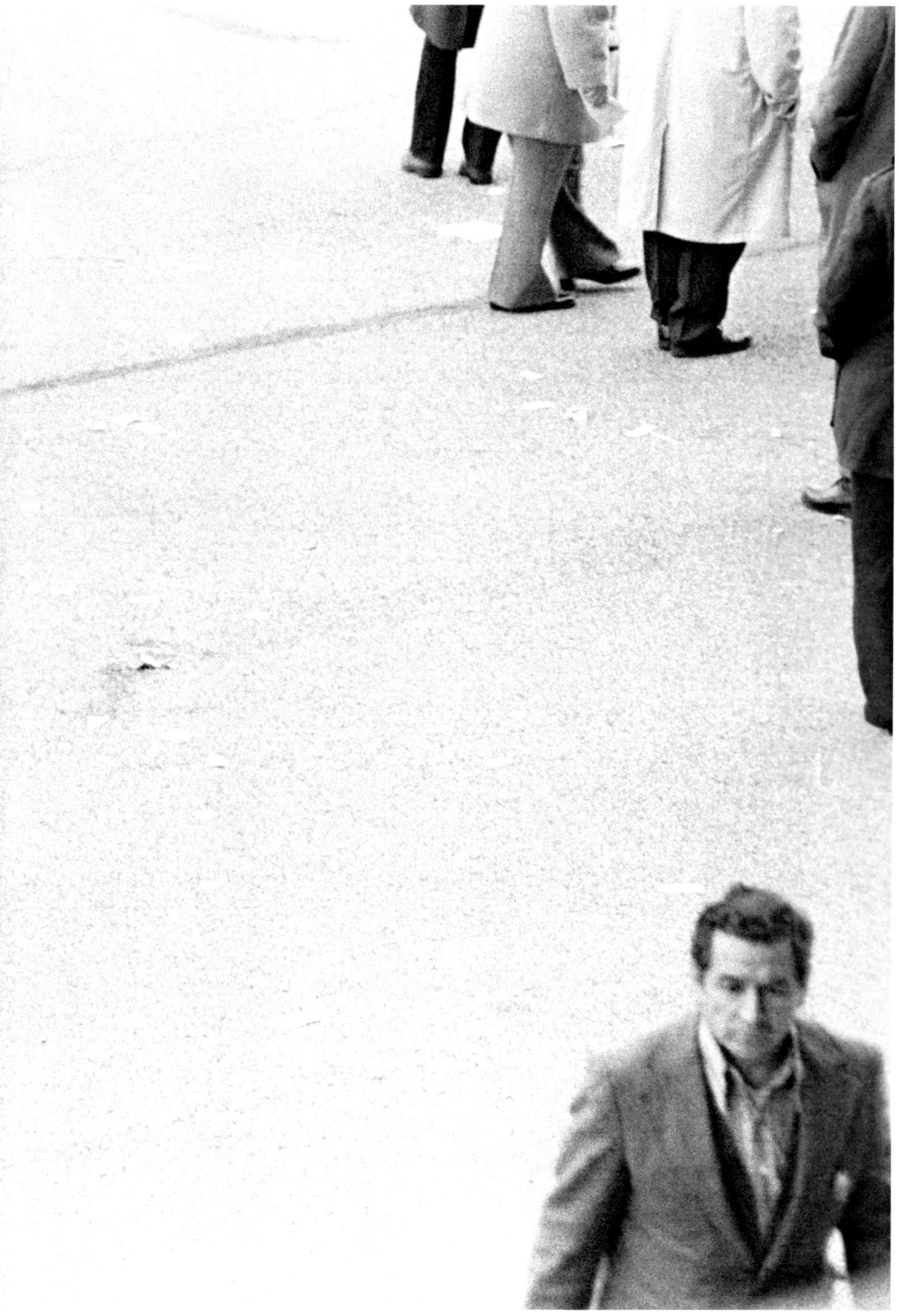

The best photo I made that day has my father smiling happily as my uncle points to a winner on his program.

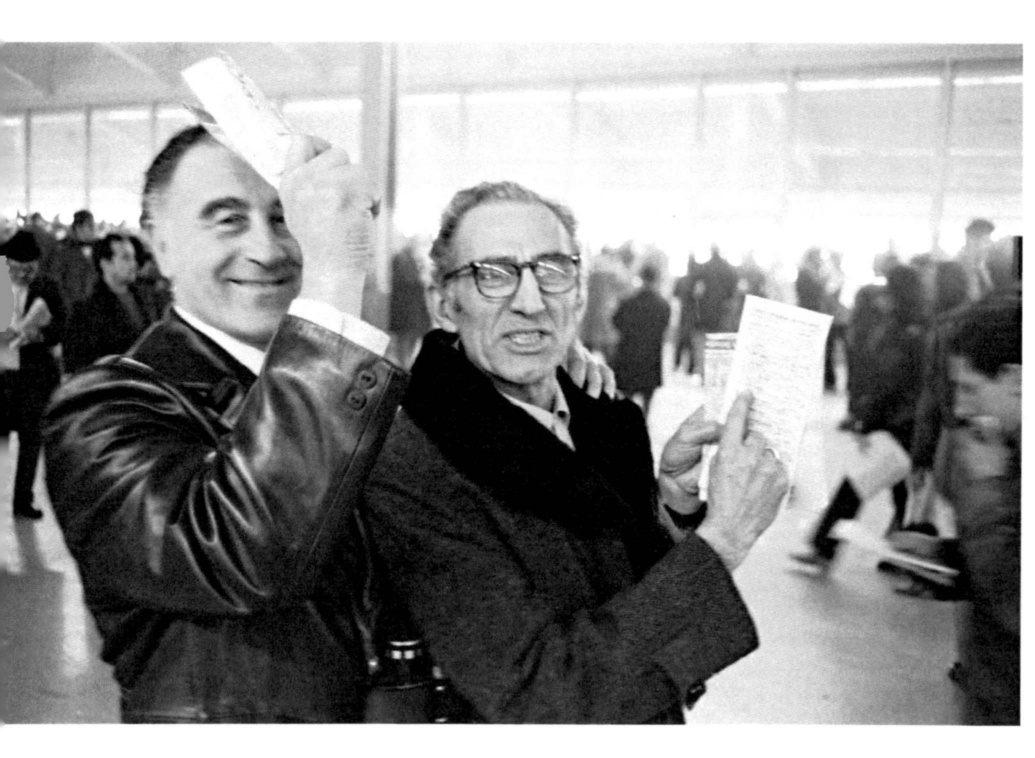

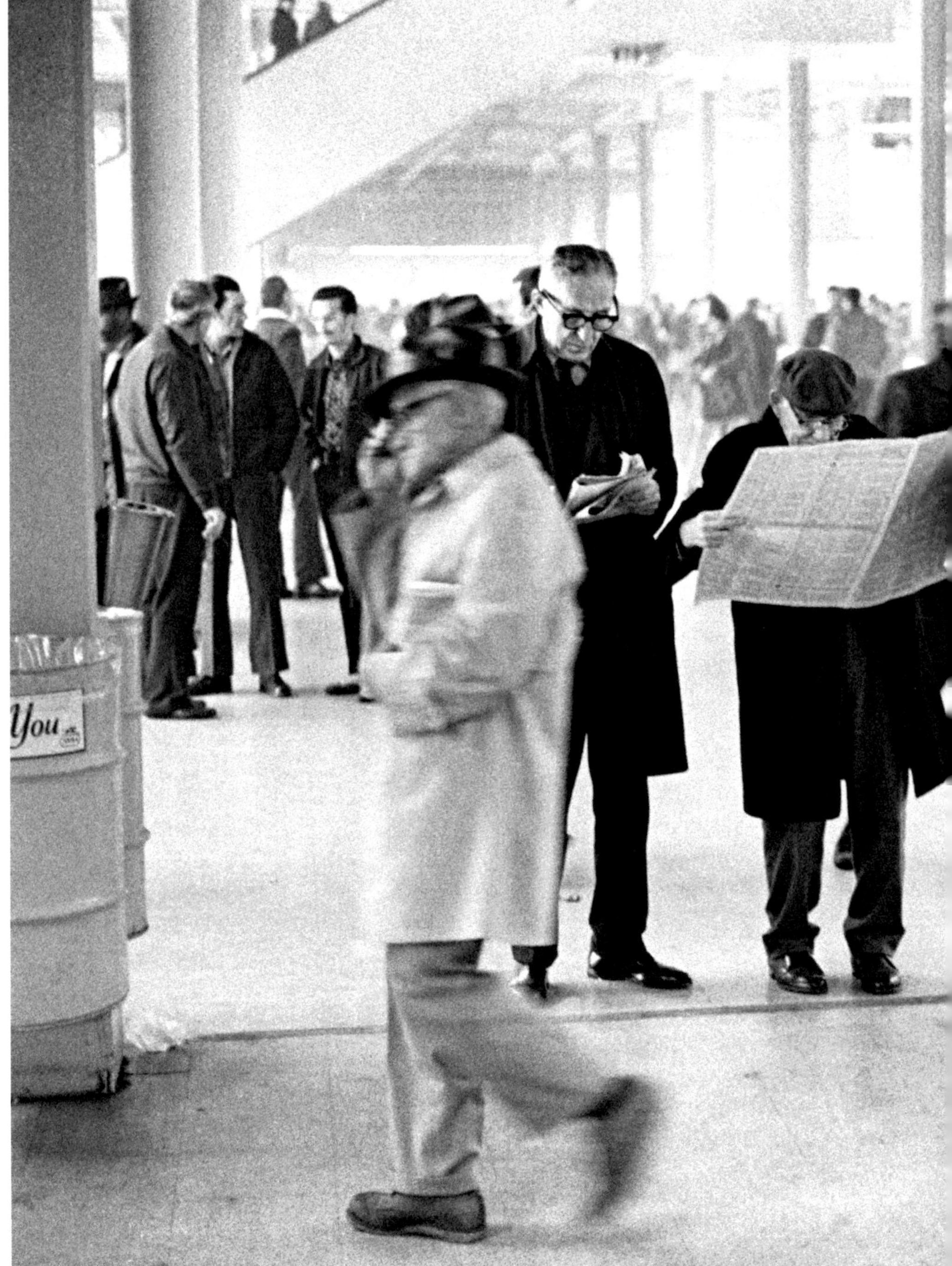

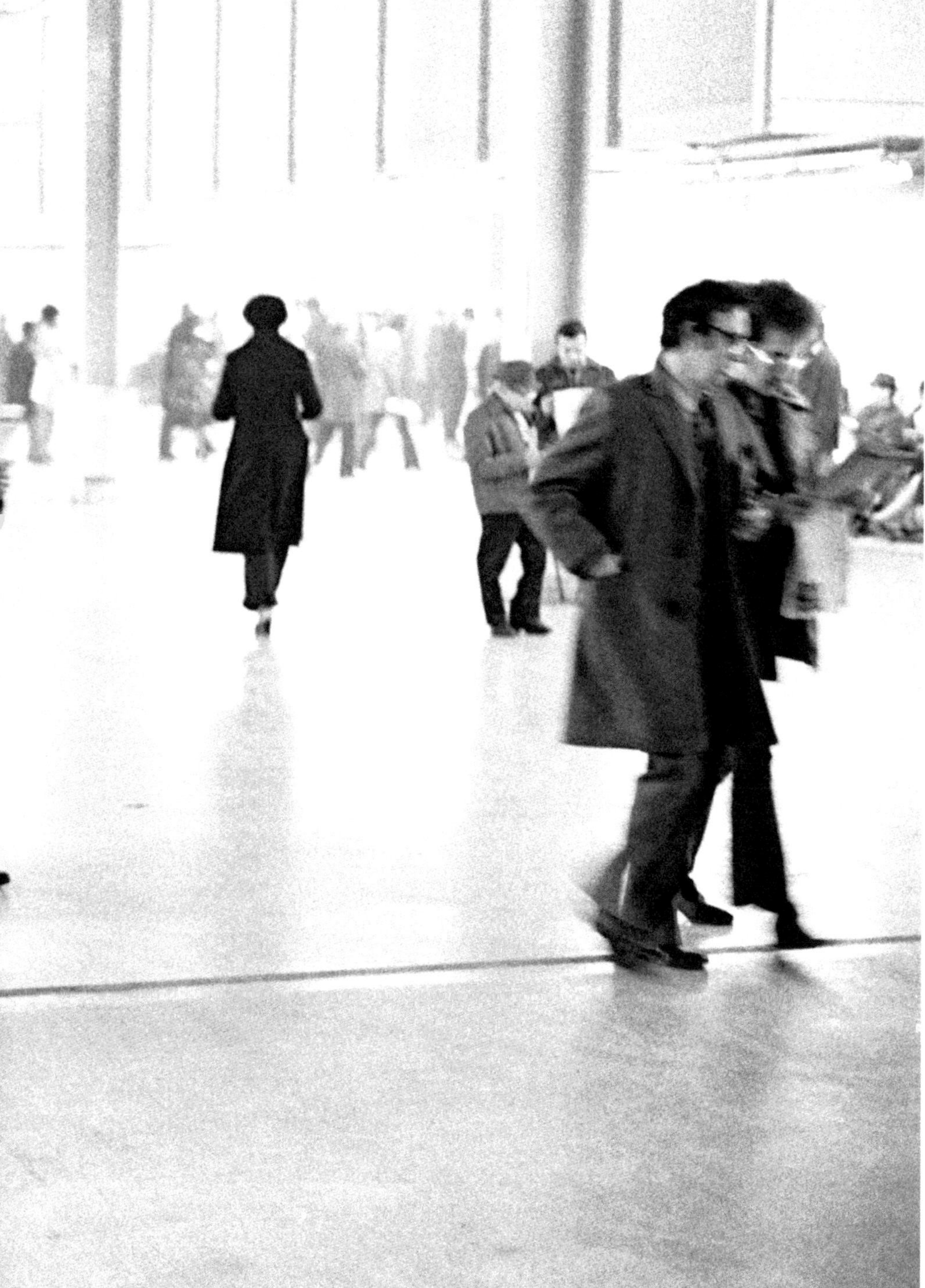

ALL AQUEDUCT NEEDS IS A POWER WASH AND A PAINT JOB:
A Day at the Big A, While It's Still Here

by JOE BIANCA

The writing is on the wall for Aqueduct Racetrack.

There has been no official announcement, but the New York Racing Association has made clear with its plans to "winterize" Belmont Park that Aqueduct, New York's stalwart winter racing home for decades, is on borrowed time. And while the logic of continuing to operate two racetracks just nine miles apart is undeniably questionable, don't let anyone fool you into thinking that nothing of value will be lost or that no one will mourn when Aqueduct becomes the latest American racing staple to bite the dust.

Opened all the way back in 1894 during a golden era when racetracks were popping up all over New York City, Aqueduct has managed to outlive them all but Belmont. The track was humbly named after a nearby conduit owned by the Brooklyn Water Works that delivered water to New York City from the Hempstead Plain. Over the years, fans have packed the Big A, as it was so nicknamed after its last major renovation project in 1959, to see the great Secretariat's retirement ceremony, the second edition of a fledgling endeavor called the Breeders' Cup, multiple Triple Crown winners, even a Pope, when John Paul II led a 75,000-strong mass on a picture-perfect autumn day in 1995.

Most importantly though, Aqueduct has long served as New York's blue-collar racetrack. Saratoga is the crown jewel of the state's racing schedule, the party destination for fans where NYRA makes the money to fund the rest of the year's operations.

Belmont has the allure of the Belmont Stakes, which, if there is a Triple Crown on the line, provides the most exciting day in our sport. It also has the distinction of housing the country's biggest racetrack and the added benefit of running during the city's most pleasant weather months.

Aqueduct, on the other hand, mostly races in the freezing cold. Situated near Jamaica Bay and John F. Kennedy Airport, the winds often make conditions even more brutal. Purse money drops. The throngs of fans and festive summer atmosphere of Saratoga could not be further away, both on the calendar and in the psyche.

But what the Aqueduct meet lacks in glamour, it makes up for in opportunity when it comes to New York's proletarian horsemen. The big barns and more decorated riders all understandably head south, mostly to Gulfstream Park in Florida, for the winter. If you can brave the harsh conditions at Aqueduct, you can compete and win races, certainly much more frequently than when Chad Brown, Todd Pletcher, Irad Ortiz, Jr., et al return north and resume their domination in the spring.

Though only separated by nine miles as the crow flies, the crowd and vibe at Aqueduct differ from the one at Belmont. The Big A is the city's track, a concrete plant residing in the working-class Queens neighborhood of Ozone Park, accessible via a $2.75 subway ride on the A express train. Belmont more resembles a giant park, lies outside of the city limits and is associated more closely with Long Island.

It's not all bad for fans of the Big A, however. Though the track's story is entering its final chapter, there still is and will be some spectacular racing at Aqueduct for the near future.

The massive renovation that began in the summer of 2022 at Belmont has now forced its racing—re-branded as Belmont at the Big A—to Aqueduct full-time. The new, smaller Belmont isn't expected to open until 2026, giving Aqueduct at least two more years in the sun.

That's the environment that brought me out to the Big A one Saturday in October 2022, shamefully my first pilgrimage on that familiar A-train ride since before the pandemic.

I met up with two of my oldest racetrack friends, Frank Henry, 35, who I went to high school with, and Sean Smith, 40, who I met through Frank dozens of track hangouts ago. As longtime Aqueduct racegoers, we knew we had to take advantage of seeing major Grade I racing at our maligned old light blue-painted friend under clear skies and comfortable fall conditions.

We posted up in our usual spot, at the far end of the second-floor grandstand, just before the clubhouse turn, among a variety of characters, mostly of West Indian and Caribbean descent. I didn't know the majority of them, but the sights, sounds and, yes, smells of the section were as comforting as a warm, increasingly tattered hoodie you bring out of the closet every winter. Slow-swaying reggae music blared from a speaker.

"This is the real Aqueduct," Henry said.

Without any prompting, the conversation quickly turned to the future of the place where we used to watch simulcasts of Saratoga before we'd ever made it through the gates of the Spa.

"All Aqueduct needs is a power wash and a paint job," said Smith, who recently moved to Ozone Park. "You have two turf courses, finally have a dirt main track [for the winter], I don't get it. I finally get a track close to my house and they want to take it away from me."

After watching eventual champion sprinter Elite Power cruise to a victory in the Grade II Vosburgh Stakes, next up was the Grade I Joe Hirsch Turf Invitational. Seeing those top-class horses run in historic Belmont-held races, I briefly had to remind myself where I was. As the horses came through the stretch for the first time in the three-turn, 1 1/2-mile Hirsch, I quickly remembered, as one especially loud fan started feverishly rooting for the leader, unaware the field had another lap to go. The crowd had a great laugh at his expense, savoring like a sweet nectar the moment when he realized they were going around again.

Following a stunning 47–1 upset in the Grade III Matron Stakes that killed any multi-race tickets we played, I went down to the first-floor bar to grab consolation beers for the crew. Naturally, there was a stereotypical animated New Yorker bragging through a heavy Brooklyn accent about having the winning horse. True to form, within a few sentences, he was off on another topic and making sure to tell everybody where he's from.

"Go-Go Gomez for [John] Terranova!" he shouted to no one in particular, getting the winning trainer right but the jockey (Eric Cancel) wrong. "Hundred-dollar horse. My boy hit the double. I might go talk to [the jockeys]. I like to go talk to them sometimes because I'm from Brooklyn. I get pictures with [Javier] Castellano. People say, 'What the fuck is the matter with you?' I say I'm from New York."

Before I headed back upstairs, I caught a hopeful glimpse of racing's future. Standing out amongst the hardened Aqueduct regulars was a group of young people, likely in their early 20s, decked out in suits and dresses. The kind of kids you usually only spot at Saratoga, taking in a day of racing at the least glamorous, but most accessible track in the city.

No, it's not Belmont and it's sure as hell not Saratoga. There are legitimate reasons why Aqueduct is mostly an afterthought. It's outdated, especially when compared to the Resorts World casino next door. It's cold. The racing quality is generally spotty.

But Aqueduct provides a raw, authentic slice of New York City, the kind that the city's ever-increasing gentrification is making harder and harder to find. That alone is worth holding onto. And rest assured, all us die-hards will hold onto it, for however long we can.

BIOS

LARRY RACIOPPO was born in South Brooklyn in 1947, and has been photographing throughout New York City since 1971. After two years in California volunteering with VISTA, he returned to New York to participate in the city's Cultural Council Foundation CETA Artists Project. He had his first solo exhibition in 1977, at Brooklyn's f stop gallery. In 1980 Scribner's published his first book of photographs, *Halloween*.

Hired in 1989 as the official photographer for the New York City Department of Housing Preservation and Development, Racioppo spent the next 22 years documenting the city's rebuilding of distressed neighborhoods. A Guggenheim Fellowship in 1997 enabled a yearlong leave of absence to develop personal projects, including a series of images that became *Forgotten Gateway: The Abandoned Buildings of Ellis Island*, a traveling exhibition originating at the National Building Museum in Washington, DC.

Racioppo's photographs are in the collections of the Museum of the City of New York; the Brooklyn Museum; the New York Public Library; the Brooklyn Public Library; El Museo del Barrio, New York; and the National September 11 Memorial & Museum, New York. Monographs include *The Word on the Street: The Photographs of Larry Racioppo* (Museum of Biblical Art, 2007), *Brooklyn Before: Photographs, 1971–1983* (Cornell University Press, 2018), and *Coney Island Baby* (2021). *Here Down on Dark Earth: Loss and Remembrance in New York City* will be released in 2025 by Fordham University Press.

JOE BIANCA is an ownership advisor for West Point Thoroughbreds, a Thoroughbred racing syndicate in racing history, which has raced horses in New York for decades. Before that, he spent seven years as a writer/editor and podcast host at *Thoroughbred Daily News*, a leading industry publication. He fell in love with the horses when New York-bred Funny Cide hit the wire first in the 2003 Kentucky Derby, carrying with him Joe's winning trifecta ticket.

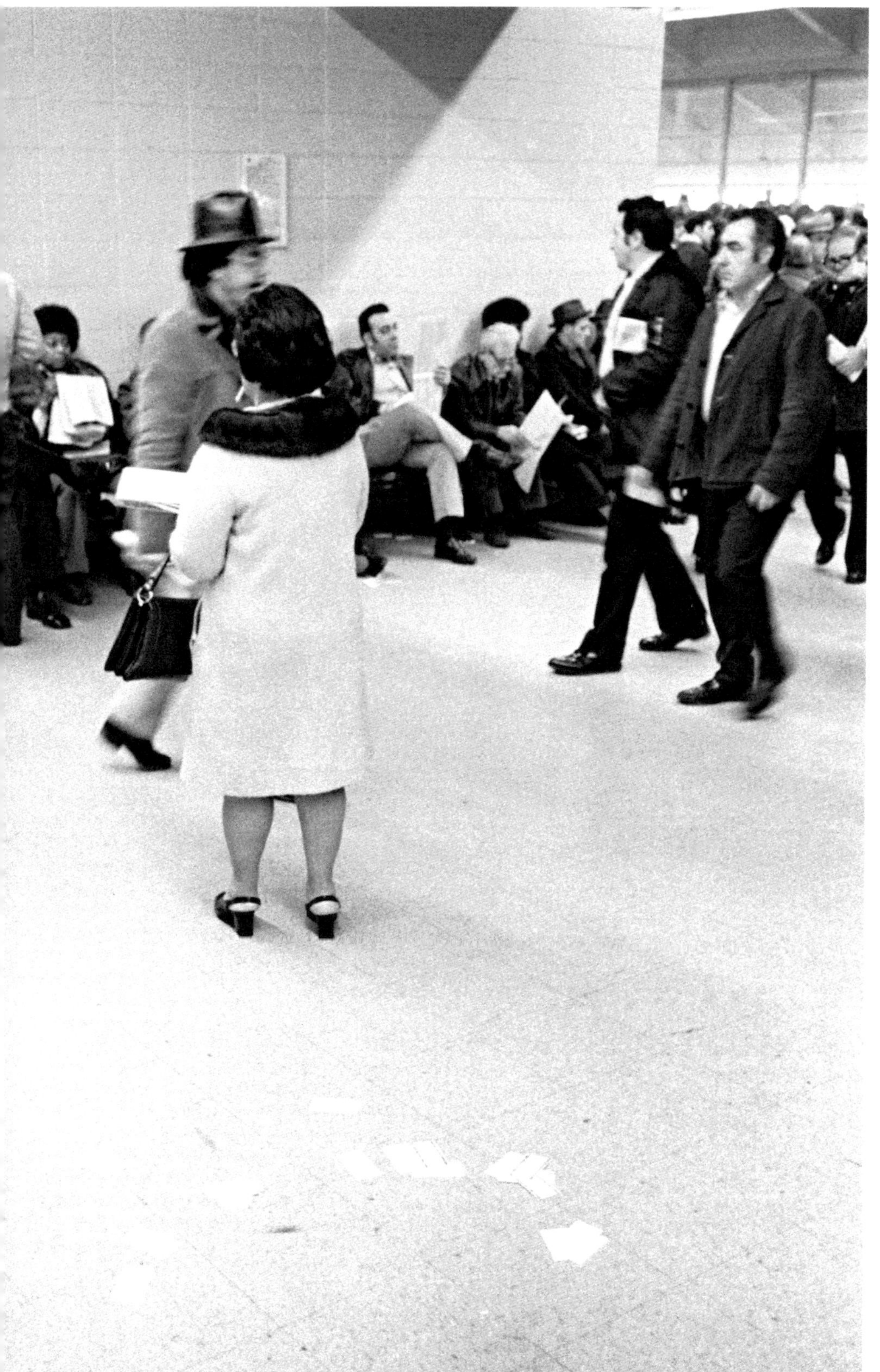

LARRY RACIOPPO
I Hope I Break Even, I Could Use The Money:
Photographs From Aqueduct Racetrack, 1972

Published by Blurring Books
@BlurringBooksNYC
Number 8 in the LSP Series

All images copyright © 2024 Larry Racioppo
Texts © 2024 Larry Racioppo and Joe Bianca
Project management by Sean M. Johnson

First Edition, First Printing of 500

Library of Congress Control Number: 2024939359
ISBN 978-1-963814-00-2
Printed in the U.K.

Book design by FRANCESCA RICHER